LIVING WITCHERY

Coven

About the author

Alexandra has been studying Western mystery traditions for over thirty years.
She is co-founder of The Circle Coven, an eclectic, women-only coven based in Australia. Her interests include Celtic mythology, Tarot and ritual practices.

Living Witchery: Coven was previously published as ***Living Witchery: From Novice to High Priestess***. Only minor changes have been made to this version.

Living Witchery: Beginner Witch Guide - written / edited by Alexandra Tanet, co-edited by Kim Fairminer and Sandra Greenhalgh will be released mid-2021.
For further information, please visit Byrningtyger.com

LIVING WITCHERY

Coven

Alexandra Tanet

© Byrning Tyger 2021
The moral rights of the author have been asserted.

All rights reserved. Except as permitted under the Australian Copyright Act 1968 (for example, a fair dealing for the purposes of study, research, criticism or review), no part of this book may be reproduced, stored in a retrieval system, communicated or transmitted in any form or by any means without prior written permission.

All inquiries should be made to the Publisher

First printed in Australia.
Ebook cover design by Kylie Sek of Cover Culture.

This book is a work of fiction. Names, characters, places, and incidents either are products of the author's imagination or are used fictitiously. Any resemblance to actual persons, living or dead, events, or locales is entirely coincidental.

ISBN 978-0-6482701-5-7

www.ByrningTyger.com

Thank you to all the wonderful, wild, wicked and wise women of The Circle Coven, past and present. Without you, this journey would have been as dust.

Thanks also to my awesome editorial support team - Kim, Gillian, Mandy and Tess. The remaining typos are evidence of my impatience rather than your skills!

Last but certainly not least, massive love to my darling husband and children for your support, encouragement and tolerance over many years. Yes, it finally did happen!

CONTENTS

Preface: Home 1
Joining a Coven 3
Thrown in the Deep End 10
First Ritual 15
Coven Politics 20
Dedication Ritual 27
A New High Priest 31
Inside Witch Rituals 37
First Degree Initiations 43
Celebrating the Wheel of the Year 49
Growing a Coven 54
Second Degree, Shadow Work and More Changes 58
Coven Re-boot 65
The Power of Three: A New Coven 68
The Circle Coven Genesis 73
A Women Only Space 79
Initiation and Women's Mysteries 85
Teaching New Witches 89
An Annus Horribilis 93
Highlights and Fun Times 101
Divination 108
Money Mojo Bag Spell 113
Epilogue: The Circle 119
Recommended Reading & Bibliography 122

PREFACE: HOME

THE CIRCLE COVEN FEELS LIKE HOME. We share laughter and stories as we sit on Scarlet's veranda after celebrating our ritual under the full moon. The mood is one of peace, contentment and connection.

We are a group of witches living in a large city in Australia. Most of the time coven members go about our usual lives of working, house cleaning, cooking food, and spending time with partners, family and friends. Together, we look like a group of normal people in ordinary clothes.

But if you listened closely, you would hear us speak of our plans for the next ritual, or the difficulties of removing candle wax from robes. Maybe we are discussing the importance of walking with bare feet upon the earth, or the outcomes of a recent tarot card reading. Despite superficial appearances, we are not so ordinary, after all.

Modern witchcraft is a vibrant spiritual practice based on the love of nature, exploration of the 'supernatural' and honoring Deity through connections with pre-Christian goddesses and gods. Witchery lore includes topics such as herb-craft, divination, spell-casting and healing.

We do not worship the devil, or do the work of Satan, or harm animals, despite the occasional sensationalized, ill-informed media release. Such things are anathema to contemporary witches.

Many witches would prefer to live in the country like our spiritual forebears, if we could still access the world via the internet.

However, the gritty reality is that most of us are urban dwellers. We consciously go about our magical practices with planes flying above us, noisy traffic beside us and bitumen beneath us. But within our concrete jungles we spend time in hidden pockets of parklands and observe the turning of the world's seasons by the nesting habits of magpies or the shedding of jacaranda blossoms in the springtime.

We perform our rituals red-robed in suburban back yards, beside tolerant neighbors, rather than deep in ancient forests. When it is cold, we meet inside a warm and cozy house. We find no disharmony in how we apply our witchcraft practices to modern day life, because a key tenet of eclectic witchcraft is to 'do whatever works.'

Witchcraft is practical and prosaic, as well as starry-eyed and otherworldly. At the heart of witchery is a mystery tradition of balance and integration, accessible to all who seek it.

JOINING A COVEN

MY LEGS WERE SHAKING as I walked up the creaking wooden stairs. The address I'd been given led me to a high-set timber house with deep verandas, located beside a busy main road. There was a heavy stench of pollution from the trucks that rumbled by, and it didn't seem a likely setting to learn about the mysteries of the universe.

I wondered if I had turned up at the wrong destination.

Quickly I re-checked my scribbled notes. Nope, I was in the right place and at the right time. This was exactly where I was supposed to be. Beyond these doors were the witches.

A few months earlier I'd posted a hand-written application to the Coven of the Silver Moon. My application included details about my time of birth and reasons for wanting to become a member of the coven. Writing down that information was a daring step into the unknown for me.

Why was I, a relatively normal twenty-something year old nurse, applying to join a witch coven? Whatever was I getting myself into? My husband and parents thought I had gone crazy. Maybe I had gone crazy. But despite their doubts, coupled with a few doubts of my own, I knew this was something that I really wanted to do.

In the early nineties, internet communication was a twinkle in the eye of elite uber-geeks. Facebook or Meetup groups didn't exist and information about witchcraft was scarce. Connecting with other people with the same interests in witchcraft or paganism required finding a savvy tarot card reader, or spending hours lurking in the occult section of quirky bookshops reading notices pinned onto a board.

Despite these challenges, I was drawn to learn more. The supernatural, spell work, magic, ESP and mythology fascinated me. Now, here I was, about to attend my first ever workshop on witchcraft.

"Hello, I'm Alexandra," I greeted the friendly Rubenesque woman who answered the door. She was dressed in a flowing green dress with fancy lace. "I'm here for the, uh, workshop."

"Ah, yeah, right. Come on in. I'm Rosemary," she gestured me into the house. "Cerridwen is in the kitchen."

Immediately, I wondered whether this was code for something I didn't understand. Perhaps I was expected to supply the second half of the passcode to her oblique statement. Alternatively, perhaps Cerridwen, the Celtic Goddess of transformation, was indeed in the back of the house.

Rosemary correctly interpreted my slightly bewildered expression.

"Cerridwen is the High Priestess, the leader of the coven" she explained slowly, "She's in the kitchen, making a pot of tea."

The High Priestess of the Coven of the Silver Moon was indeed making a pot of tea in the kitchen. She was a small woman with long straight dark hair, and eyes outlined with a remarkable amount of kohl and mascara. I felt tall and awkward as I repeated my mantra of my name and that I was here for the, uh, workshop.

"Welcome, Alexandra," she replied in an earthy voice, looking intently at me. "We are glad that you could join us. Would you like a cuppa?"

Cerridwen radiated intensity, despite her prosaic offer of a cup of tea, and I felt subdued all over again. Was she reading my mind? Did she know how nervous I was?

It was difficult to work out what she was thinking beneath the heavy mask of eye makeup. I gratefully accepted the tea cup, and then fled from her presence to join the people who were already waiting.

Eventually, eight of us were sitting in the large, haphazardly decorated lounge room. The experienced witches and Novices (as new members were referred to) seemed as uniquely attired as the house furnishings, with clothing ranging from colorful hippy to monochrome black to op-shop mix-up to boring conservative. Of course, I was the only one in boring conservative soccer-mum clothing, a situation that would repeat numerous times over the next few decades. I felt a little out of place, but no one else seemed to mind my fashion choices.

Everyone seemed very friendly, despite the hot, humid temperature of an Australian summer afternoon. The ceiling fans whirred with some efficiency and occasionally a gust of hot wind wafted in through the open windows as we waited for everyone to arrive. The constant traffic noises did nothing to dim my enthusiasm, or my nerves.

We waited. And waited.

The experienced witches tried to explain the delay, while Cerridwen sat in serene silence and sipped her tea.

"George likes to walk everywhere, so he loses track of things. He's on Pagan Time."

"We can't start without George. He has all the lesson notes. I'm sure he'll be here soon."

"George is bringing his drum. We need the drum, for the meditation. George is a great drummer."

"Ah, Sarah should be here soon too I think. She won't be too far away..."

That day I learnt an important lesson about this thing called 'Pagan Time.' Essentially, Pagan Time occurs when there is a significant degree of flexibility between the planned commencement time and when people arrive or start the actual event. As a nurse who is used to timing actions exactly to minutes or to seconds, and by nature being quite impatient, I found Pagan Time a difficult concept. Everyone else seemed relaxed about waiting for the latecomers, including George and his drum, so I did my best to keep my impatience hidden.

While we waited, the experienced witches talked about the history of the Coven of the Silver Moon. They had formed this new collective after deciding to break away from an older coven, where they'd been members for many years. There was no animosity towards their old coven; they just wanted a change of focus. The experienced witches were keen to train new members to learn about their witchcraft practices and bring up the number of coveners to thirteen in total.

Cerridwen then invited us Novices to talk about ourselves and explain why we were here today. She asked us about what attracted us to this non-mainstream spiritual path.

To me, witchcraft is enthralling. It's the subject of countless books and movies, and is embedded in ancient mythology as well as common culture. While historical (and Biblical) accounts often portray The Witch as evil and something to be feared, avoided or punished, modern witches do not see themselves in such a manner. In contrast to early modern European accusations, contemporary witches don't waste precious time by poisoning the crops, causing the milk to curdle or making women infertile.

Instead of consorting with the Devil, modern witches share a love of connecting with the natural world. We explore cosmologies of the Other-worlds – the so called 'supernatural' - and are drawn to practices such as divination, healing, and meditation.

Like our historical forebears, we may work magic in the form of spell-work, though this is usually performed with good intentions, rather than to cause harm.

This isn't the magic of Harry Potter, where a wave of a wand and a few words will produce fire balls or eerie creatures. This is the magic of directed will-power harnessed with intangible energies of earth, sun and moon to create a manifested result. It's also the magic of synchronicities, harmony and interconnectedness between beings.

Each of the Novices agreed that none of us deliberately chose to 'become' a witch. Instead, we independently came to the realization that is what, or who, we are. Some used the words Wicca and Witchcraft interchangeably, although they have slightly different meanings, as Wicca is one specific kind of witchcraft tradition. But the words Wicca or Witch seemed to best describe our shared belief systems and practices.

✷ ✷ ✷

When George (and his drum) finally arrived, the first workshop lesson commenced. The topic was based around the history of witchcraft, to help us learn more about our spiritual path. We heard of some key people involved in the development of Wicca, such as Gerald Gardner, who is called the Father of Witchcraft; Alex Sanders; the 'Great Beast' Aleister Crowley; Dion Fortune; and Doreen Valiente.

Cerridwen also discussed how magical practices from Freemasonry, the Order of the Golden Dawn and Thelema were melded with ancient European and Egyptian traditions to create the 'flavor' of witchcraft that the coven followed. She warned that there are considerable variances in how people practice witchcraft in contemporary society, as there is no one leader to dictate how things should be done.

This lack of leadership allows a lot of diversity but has led to some furious exchanges between practitioners of different magical traditions. She suggested that we should be very careful to avoid entering fights about which witch is which, or the best.

I thought this was good advice, as I wasn't interested in starting any arguments with someone who could consider a curse as an appropriate response to a verbal disagreement.

George then shared the magic of drumming with us, beating out the rhythm on his round-framed drum as we learnt witchy chants and songs together. We found how the vibrations from a drum beat can affect our bodies and mind, so I was quite grateful for George's (slightly tardy) contributions to the workshop.

But the best aspect of the afternoon was simply being able to spend time with people who shared the same interests that I did, and asking all the burning questions that I hadn't been able to ask anyone else previously. I simply loved the company of other witches. Talking about the non-mundane and deeper aspects of life with other people satisfied my soul.

Finally, the workshop came to an end as the harsh daylight turned to shadows. It was time to go back to our everyday lives. The experienced witches seemed tired and dispirited by the end of the day. When we left, I was fare-welled with a casual, "See you later."

I wasn't invited to any follow-up meetings or workshops, although I saw a few whispered conversations happening around the room. But no one talked to me about any future coven events.

I felt a distinct sense of anti-climax.

As I walked down the stairs, I felt like I'd been given a glimpse into this world of witchery and it seemed like it was over already. Maybe I'd failed some kind of secret test that I didn't know about? Maybe I'd laughed too much at the wrong time or been too bossy?

I went home and agonized, waiting for a phone call or letter inviting me to the next coven event.

It was a long wait.

Weeks and weeks later, I found out the reasons for the lack of contact and follow-up. I hadn't failed some arcane test. The reasons were far more straightforward. Cerridwen, the High Priestess, had accepted a new overseas job, and a couple of the other experienced witches had relocated away from the city, leaving the coven in a state of flux.

I hadn't been deemed unworthy at all, as it was simply a case of coven membership changes. What a huge relief.

A woman named Domino, who hadn't attended the workshop, phoned me and let me know what had happened. She invited me to a meeting at her house in a week's time, to discuss forming a new coven. I was thrilled to be included, and marked down the date in my calendar with a big red circle with lots of exclamation marks.

THROWN IN THE DEEP END

IT WAS A RAUCUS TRIP to my second coven meeting. This time, I wouldn't be nervously walking alone into a strange house, wondering who and what awaited me. On the way to Domino's house, I car-pooled in the company of a couple of witches called Rhea and Jonathan. We had all been strangers until about twenty minutes ago. Now we were all the best of friends, brought together by our shared interests.

Domino's house was located in a bayside suburb close to the city. It was a double-story, brick building on a large flat block with a pool in the backyard. In many ways, it was a typical suburban estate house, until you got close enough to see the enormous pentagram painted on the front door, with a couple of carved stone gargoyles at the gate.

A pentagram is a five-pointed star encompassed by a circle. This symbol (with one point at the top) is frequently worn by pagans and witches as a form of magical protection, or as an identifying symbol of their spiritual beliefs, in a similar way to how Christians might have a fish sticker on their car-bumper, or wear a cross pendant around their necks.

An inverted pentagram (with two points at the top) is flaunted by some Satanists and heavy metal music aficionados, so a pentagram can seem quite a confronting shape to people unaware of the significance of the different shapes. To make things more complex, an inverted pentagram may be worn by experienced witch initiates in some Wiccan traditions.

Domino's house paraded the upright pentagram symbol with pride and we knew we had arrived at the correct address.

Domino met us at the door. If the pentagram wasn't a clear indication that there was a witch living inside, any residual doubts were put aside when she greeted us. Around her neck she wore a mass of tangled silver chains - including the ubiquitous pentagram pendant- and she had long black hair, colorful tattoos and was dressed in flowing dark clothing. She was very welcoming and made us feel immediately at home, ushering us up the staircase.

There were probably about twenty people crowded into the upstairs lounge room by the time everyone arrived, according to their own interpretation of Pagan Time. Of course, as I was driving the car, we were there exactly at the time specified, though I did my best to try and be a little bit late, so I could fit in with this strange pagan culture.

I was slightly reassured when I found my new friend Rhea shared my dislike of Pagan Time. She was also a nurse and stickler for punctuality. Sadly, not everyone shared our love of being on time.

The lounge room was noisy, with tobacco smoke drifting about and cups of tea or coffee being offered freely. As per the time-honored Australian tradition everyone brought a plate, which is to say that everyone brought food to share, so there was a varied feast to be had, most of which was quite unhealthy.

This was not a gathering of quiet, peaceful and serene folk who blissfully gazed at navels and ate vegan food, contrary to my previous expectations! I was, incidentally, one of the minority (of two people) who didn't smoke cigarettes.

These witches were loud and passionate, yet somehow everyone managed to have their say and voice their opinions. There were a lot of discussions about what went wrong with the Coven of the

Silver Moon, as well as the older coven (the Golden Sun Coven) and how things could have been done better. Most people had been a member of one - or both - of these covens, though it seemed that over all these witches lacked the years of experience of those who taught at the Coven of the Silver Moon workshop.

Although I'd only attended one Novice workshop, I felt confident to voice my views in this raucous yet accepting group. When it was my time to speak, I shared that for the past few years I'd been undertaking the wonderful correspondence course run by The Order of Bards, Ovates and Druids. I'd also lived in England for a year, visiting the sacred sites and reading everything I could get my hands on about Druidry, witchcraft and magic.

The other witches seemed impressed by my overseas adventures, and I was very pleased to think that I didn't sound too much like the newcomer that I was.

After a lot of talking, many of the witches in the room were committed to creating a new coven. Other witches wished to stay members of the Golden Sun Coven, but all agreed that the Coven of the Silver Moon was no more, after brief but promising beginnings. Following more debate, we all agreed on a brand-new name for our brand-new witch coven.

The Coven of the Enchanted Cauldron was born!

That night, another decision was made that had a huge impact on my life. All those present who wished to create the new coven were invited to join what was called the 'Inner Circle' of the Coven of the Enchanted Cauldron. This included me, who had only attended one Novice workshop. But sometimes, life is about turning up and being in the right place at the right time. This was one of those occasions.

Within our inherited coven tradition, the Inner Circle includes the experienced witches who teach the lessons, make decisions and assist the High Priestess and High Priest in running the coven. However, due to the more egalitarian nature of this brand-new coven, there was no appointed High Priestess or High Priest, so the Inner Circle members would be the folk in charge.

Being asked to join the Inner Circle was a huge step up for me, particularly as this was only my second coven gathering. Suddenly I'd gone from rank raw Novice at the first workshop, to someone on the 'inside.' But, like many witches of that time, I had spent years reading (and re-reading) every book I could get my hands on, so I did have some theoretical 'head-knowledge.'

I put most of my success down to how fantastic I am at bluffing and appearing confident in a range of unexpected situations. I'd somehow managed to convince the other witches that I had enough experience to assist in forming the new coven, and they didn't realize how little practical experience I had.

That night I was fascinated to learn about the personalities of the other Inner Circle members, as we spent the second part of the night chatting about our plans for the new coven. There was eleven of us in total, including Rhea (my car-pool nurse buddy) and Domino, our host.

Little did I know that one year later there would only be three Inner Circle members left in the coven.

One of the first duties of the newly established Inner Circle was to decide which lucky people would be our new Novices. We'd inherited the hand-written forms from eleven applicants, and we passed these around the room, so everyone could read why these strangers wanted to learn about witchcraft. There was no vetting process. We boldly agreed to accept all the applicants as Novices.

Following on from that weighty decision of choosing our new members, we each inherited jobs to do. I was blessed with the responsibility of typing up the curriculum for Novice lessons, which were based on our discussions that night as well as the old coven's program.

As this was the mid-1990s, computers were a rare novelty, but I'd recently taught myself some basic word processing skills and I was lucky enough to have access to a computer and printer in my workplace. This was the time when computer documents were saved onto big black floppy discs that were actually floppy.

Usually, an electronic typewriter was as sophisticated as it got for crafting most of the coven documentation. Much of our paperwork from those days was handwritten, then photocopied at a local library. Computer generated notes were quite the luxury, and I was pleased to assist.

That night I learned that running a coven requires a lot of behind the scenes administration work. One necessity is to create a contact list.

Back in the mid-Nineties there were no mobile phones smaller than a toaster, so multiple pieces of paper were handed around from person to person that night, with everyone writing their home address and landline phone number. From that information, we developed our telephone tree, which is a quaint process of working out who would ring who, and then who that person would contact in turn to ensure everyone was in touch with each other.

Driving away from my second coven meeting was a satisfying experience. I didn't have any of that sense of let-down that I felt after the first witchcraft workshop. This time I felt a sense of purpose, of solidarity and excitement. I was the member of a fantastic new coven, and on the verge of a wonderful journey.

FIRST RITUAL

THE COVEN OF THE ENCHANTED CAULDRON – quickly abbreviated to TEC for convenience - was off to a roaring start, with eleven members of the Inner Circle (including yours truly) and eleven new Novices. Like its predecessor covens, TEC was a teaching coven, with lessons delivered on a weekly basis as well during weekend workshops.

All the Inner Circle members nominated to teach different subjects to the Novices, and our curriculum included a wealth of foundational topics such as the Eightfold Wheel of the Year, divination, and crystals. In many ways, our curriculum was similar to any generic witchcraft book, but books can't replace face-to-face teaching, when students can ask questions and discuss topics of special interest.

The coven curriculum diligently excluded any spell-craft lessons for the first few months. The more experienced witches advised that this is a very sound practice as it deters people who wish to join a coven simply so that they can learn to curse someone they don't like, or place a love spell on someone that they do like but who doesn't reciprocate their feelings. Careful lesson planning also provides a teaching coven enough time to help inexperienced people learn the fundamentals of witchcraft, expected behavior and ethical practices.

Most coven nights, the 'lowly Novices' would have their lessons in the downstairs lounge room, while the Inner Circle members would meet upstairs to chat, smoke and eat. I can't remember too much higher learning happening in the elevated room of the Inner

Circle, though there certainly was a lot of gossiping and merriment. Regardless of that, I certainly felt very wise being there, learning through osmosis and listening to interesting witchy conversations.

The stand-out advantage to being a member of the elite Inner Circle was that I could participate in coven rituals, unlike the new Novices who first needed to complete six months of preparatory lessons.

Witches usually celebrate two main kinds of rituals; Sabbats and Esbats. Sabbats are celebrated each Equinox and Solstice and at the in-between cross quarter times of the year. Esbats are celebrated once a month at the time of the full moon. These full moon rituals are a time to perform magic and connect with the lunar energies of the Goddess.

I still remember my joy at being invited to my first Esbat ritual, which was to be held in Domino's backyard. When the date was set, I went home and frantically read everything I could on how to perform a ritual, so that the other Inner Circle members wouldn't guess I'd never participated in a witch's Esbat. I felt nervous because my theoretical knowledge would soon be put to a practical test, but I prepared as best as I could.

I dug a long, loose black kimono out of the depths of my cupboard to stand-in for a robe, fasted with only water to drink after breakfast, scrubbed my body with salted water and prepared a plate of food to share after our ritual.

Right... I was ready!

One of the surprising things I learnt that first full moon ritual was what witches wore under their robes. Perhaps there is a Scottish connection, in addition to the three witches in Shakespeare's Macbeth, because under our robes we wore what Scotsmen purportedly wear under their kilts. Nothing. At. All.

Along with ritual clothing requirement was the other slightly surprising concept of everyone stripping off and getting robed up in the same room, with no gender separation. This wasn't as awkward as it sounds, as everyone just did their own thing and ignored what bodily parts were on display around them.

Witches aren't by nature prudish, or ashamed of our physical bodies, which is a refreshing change from a body-judging society. In later years, we would perform sky-clad rituals, when no one wore any clothes at all. Participating in these rituals actually felt quite liberating once the initial nervousness wore off!

After getting robed-up, we walked quietly down to the ritual space – 'the circle'– dodging the huge mounds of dog excreta from Domino's three huge dogs. The circle was in a corner of the yard, fringed by trees and a herb garden.

In that round space, we placed special ritual items (including a bell, an incense burner spilling out fumes of glorious smelling frankincense, two large candles and a glass goblet filled with honey mead) onto a card-table covered in black velvet drapes. When the preparations were completed, we sat cross legged on the earth and meditated together under the stars until it was time to begin.

My first coven ritual was quite unlike anything I'd ever done before. It was bewildering and wonderful, both at the same time.

I didn't know where to stand, or where things went, what to say, or what I should be doing at the correct time. I simply continued in my previous mock-confident bluffing style, and quietly watched the experienced witches before mimicking everything that they did.

I don't think I did anything too obviously wrong...I think. If anyone glared at me because I mucked something up, the night was too dark to see any facial expressions underneath the other witches' shadowy hoods.

The ritual included a lot of dramatic waving around of short daggers (athames); proclaiming at unseen entities at the cardinal points; declaiming “thous” and “thees;” walking around the ritual space in a clockwise direction; and beseeching of the God (the masculine principle of Deity) and the Goddess (the female principle of Deity).

We drank honeyed mead, passing around the cup so we all sipped from the same vessel, and shared some very delicious homemade biscuits.

It was a simply amazing experience.

At the end of the ritual, the rulers of the Elemental Kingdoms of Earth, Air, Fire and Water were “hailed and fair-welled” back into their “lovely realms.” My first ritual was over, though I didn’t want it to end.

* * *

There is far more to participating in a witchy ritual than what I had read about in my books. The sense of the numinous, the intense, shared focus by everyone involved, and all the single components which made up the greater ritual affected me deeply.

I loved it, despite not understanding a lot of what was going on, or the reasons for some of the actions or words.

For the first time, I really understood why shared rituals are integral to a witch coven. Although it’s enjoyable to participate with others in a chosen activity, this witchy ritual was not the same as sharing a Monopoly board game. A coven ritual is much more than just chatting with others who have similar interests.

In a magical ritual, our normal, everyday state of consciousness changes and we access different states of ‘being’ and ‘knowing.’

We escape from distracting thoughts of everyday life, such as work, children, grocery lists or washing the clothes.

A group ritual provides a designated time and place where our attention is firmly directed towards the subtler dimensions. This is the 'space' where magic is generated, and we can be open to a sense of union with the Divine. And all of that is what I felt during my first coven Esbat celebration.

After the ritual, we sat around the fire, sharing food and stories. We laughed and were solemn. We talked about the ritual, the Universe and our lives. That night, I said what many other people new to a coven have expressed to me numerous times over the years: "I feel like I have come home."

That's the amazing sensation you experience when you join a coven and connect with the members, and the egregore (the 'group soul') reaches out to embrace you. You feel like you have come home after travelling in hostile lands, and these people in the magical circle with you are your new family. Your new family is one connected to you by spirit rather than by blood or marital certificate.

I felt blessed to have found such a wonderful group of like-minded witches and sit with them on the grass under the shining full moon. As I tipped a small amount of mead from my cup onto the earth, I gave thanks for the good luck to have found the perfect coven.

COVEN POLITICS

AFTER MY FIRST RITUAL with the Coven of the Enchanted Cauldron, I left Domino's home feeling as if I was floating on top of the world. For the next few days, I felt energized and vibrant. I could hardly wait until next week's meeting to spend more time with my newly found coven family.

I was simply the most fortunate witch, ever.

But, lo, how the mighty doth fall.

Judy, one of the older and more experienced Inner Circle members, had never been particularly fond of me. Sadly, over time she became more and more set in her adversarial mind-set. Although I thought she was nice enough, though slightly eccentric, I later found that she passionately detested me and spoke bitterly against me being in the Inner Circle.

It eventually turned into a major personality clash, though I wasn't aware of the degree of her dislike for me until after our first ritual together.

One of my main crimes, among the many others that I was apparently guilty of, was that I wasn't a 'real' witch. More significantly, I was the only one of the Inner Circle members who hadn't been an initiated member of either of the previous covens and was therefore an anomaly.

Unknown to me, the very determined Judy had instigated a lot of 'back room' conversation after my first coven ritual. When I turned up to the routine lesson the following week, I found that I had been kicked out of the coven.

Or rather, I had been kicked downstairs, to join the lower-class citizens who were the Novices.

I believe that Judy's preference was for me to be removed from the coven altogether, but fortunately she didn't get her way on everything she wanted. Domino and Rhea, who were closer to me in age and attitude, spoke up on my behalf. But Judy had greater authority in the coven hierarchy and I was banished from the Inner Circle.

I was furious.

I was hurt.

I was seething with resentment.

The lessons the Novices were receiving from the Inner Circle members included topics that I had read about years ago and were therefore nothing new to me. These were lessons I should have been teaching rather than receiving.

I was in a world of hurt ego and bruised self-righteousness, and the only things that kept me from immediately leaving the coven were the kindness and friendship of Rhea, who remained in the Inner Circle, and my own bloody-minded determination.

Instead of the coven being a place of sanctuary, socializing and fun, it became a dreary place of stained carpets and cockroach-infested cupboards. Novices weren't allowed upstairs – we even had segregated tea and coffee facilities in our own loungeroom - and I would be bitter all over again when I heard the laughter of the Inner Circle members wafting down the stairs.

On the nights of coven meetings, I would turn up shamefaced at the pentagrammed door, and then sit in petulance during the lessons given by the Inner Circle witches, who had been my close peers such a short time ago.

Rhea, who had car pooled with me on our first trip to Domino's house, helped keep me sane during that difficult time. She is a power-pack of five-foot-nothing with long henna-red hair, a very keen wit and an equally keen sense of justice. She disagreed with everything that Judy had to say, but ultimately Judy's sheer aggression and subversive tactics had won out.

We would meet up for coffee, as Rhea loves her coffee - the bigger the better - and she let me know how some Inner Circle members (herself included) were arguing to have me reinstated. Judy, however, was intransigent in her passionate dislike of me.

Rhea also found out that Judy had a track record of seemingly irrationally disliking someone, and then getting them expelled from the group. Apparently, I was just the most recent person in a long line of targets. Knowing that information did salve my ego and make me feel slightly better about my situation.

This was my first venture into 'coven politics.' and it certainly wouldn't be my last experience. Interpersonal issues such as this are the reason why many people leave a coven, or don't wish to join one in the first place.

Coven membership can create a whole new world of hurt, with some people repeating the same immature behaviors they demonstrated in kindergarten. Those negative behaviors seem amplified when personality mismatches occur in a small group of people. There is a lot of emotional pain for everyone involved.

It was a tough call deciding whether I should leave, or stay with the coven and work through my emotions of hurt and rejection towards a positive outcome. I chose the second option, most likely because of stubbornness more than anything else.

Eventually, Rhea navigated a great solution. She decided that I should undergo a Dedication ritual. Completing a Dedication ritual would make me a 'formal' member of the coven and put me on an even footing with the other Inner Circle members who had already completed a Dedication ritual with their previous coven. Then Judy would have no firm grounds at all for my expulsion from the Inner Circle because I "wasn't a witch."

I clapped my hands together in excitement at the thought of being involved in a witchy Initiation ritual, and paid for another coffee for Rhea.

※ ※ ※

But this all took a while, and in the meantime, I turned up weekly and despondently for my lessons downstairs with the other Novices. With the benefit of hindsight, being expelled from the Inner Circle was one of the best things that happened to me. After a few lessons, I began to relax and get to know a bit more about the other Novices. I started having fun, and joking around again. I even managed to like the Novices better than most of the Inner Circle members, particularly those who had voted me out!

The young and gorgeous Karina, as well as the older and slightly eccentric Lynn discovered I had a car, so I began driving them to and from coven meetings. These trips, with the three of us together, became a highlight of my week. During each journey, Karina would update us on how her many suitors tried to woo her, and Lynn would share her quite bizarre folk beliefs.

Lynn claimed to be a hereditary witch and had a virtual broom-closet full of tips and techniques inherited from her grandmother. I'm convinced she made some of these up. Regardless of the origins of some of her tales, I can't think about chicken eyes in the same way after listening to one of her stories.

There was the glamorous and emotionally fragile Elspeth. She later became a phone sex worker, which evolved into her becoming a prostitute until she met the love of her life, who asked her to leave the coven and become a Christian.

The two Charlottes were both delightful though completely different in personality, one rarely speaking and the other rarely quiet.

Deirdre loved Michael Jackson, though I was never particularly fond of her (nor she of me). She was a very close friend of Domino's, and I suspected her of tittle-tatting several times.

Gabrielle, the medievalist friend of Scarlet's, had a life which went through twists similar to a penny-dreadful novel.

Finally, in that abundance of womanhood, we had two male Novices, Robert and Anthony. Both were very fond of conspiracy theories and UFOs. Naturally, their favorite show was The X Files.

During my ostracism from the Inner Circle, most importantly, I started what would be a life-long friendship with Scarlet and Meredith.

Scarlet takes the greatest of delight telling all and sundry how much she hated me when she first met me. She thought I was egotistical, opinionated and arrogant. She was probably right.

I was licking the wounds from a giant blow to my self-image, and I certainly felt that I was far superior to the Novices. Yet here I was, lying on the dirty carpet with the Novices as we performed guided meditations. I'm sure that during that time I was far more insufferable than I normally was!

Scarlet, Meredith and I are physically very different. Whereas I am tall with long blonde hair and generous proportions, Meredith is small, neat with short curly brown hair. Scarlet is mid-height, full-bodied and her hair is everything from cropped nit-proof-short to long and vibrant red, or be-wigged.

Our personalities are different as well. Meredith has a librarian's fanaticism for everything to be exactly in its place and color coded, while I am distinctly untidy. Housework was (and still is) low on my priority list. I like to label my lack of compulsive obsessive disorder as 'creative messiness.' While Meredith and I were content with spending time by ourselves, Scarlet is an energic ball of crazy complexity and a true extrovert who hates to be alone.

Somehow the three of us clicked, despite me being prickly and unapproachable because of my Inner Circle rejection. Maybe it was because we are each 'high performers,' liking to excel in whatever we do. Maybe it is because we share a silly sense of fun.

During my time being a Novice, the seed of the friendship between Scarlet, Meredith and I began to grow sturdy roots, which has lasted the tests of time. This wasn't the case for the other new members.

Of the eleven Novices, only eight would go on to complete their First Degree Initiation the next year. Apart from Scarlet and Meredith, I have no idea where any of the others from that Novice group are today.

Some friendships last just a season, some last for years. But at the time this Novice group was my newest non-blood family and, as we met at least once a week, I saw them more frequently than some of my own by-blood family members.

DEDICATION RITUAL

RHEA HELPED PREPARE ME for my Dedication Ritual. She explained that in our coven tradition, Dedication is the first of four Rites (or rituals) of Passage. It is followed by First Degree Initiation at least a year and a day afterwards, then Second Degree and finally Third Degree Initiation. It could take years for a witch to achieve Third Degree status, as each Rite of Passage requires certain achievements and specialized study to be completed. Each one of these ceremonies marks a stage, or milestone, in a witch's spiritual journey.

During the Dedication ritual, the Novice affirms their chosen spiritual path in the presence of coven members. I was also thrilled to learn that as part of TEC's Dedication ritual, I could choose my own personal magical witch name. This is the name that other coveners would call me in recognition of my new status.

I was warned by Rhea that it was considered bad form to choose the name of a goddess or god for one's magical name. Doing so might imply ego driven arrogance or bring dynamics into my life that may not be very positive. After all, many of the pagan gods and goddesses were less than perfect beings with tumultuous lives.

So, I steered away from any existing Deity names, and after much reflection I created the Celtic-derived name of Dyffeg.

During her prep-talks, Rhea advised me that the details of Dedication and Initiation rituals are things that we must never talk about, except to other people who have completed the same ritual. Some aspects of these Rites of Passage aren't committed to paper but are passed on verbally to keep secret that which should be kept secret.

She emphasized that a Rite of Passage, either Dedication or Initiation ritual, is something that needs to be experienced, rather than read from a book while sitting in a comfy chair.

Performed properly, and at the proper time for the initiate, Rites of Passage can channel subtle forces which are literally life changing. When the person undergoing the ritual doesn't know in advance what will occur, this adds to the mystery and impact of the ritual.

The initiate therefore needs to be ready to openly accept and embrace the experience they are about to undergo, and trust in the people who are coordinating the ritual. Additionally, they need to have the self-confidence to trust themselves, and their own reactions to unexpected circumstances. These are some meanings behind the frequently used phrase: "perfect love and perfect trust."

Bearing all that in mind, what I will share about my first Rite of Passage is how it deviated slightly from the expected format.

On the night of my Dedication ritual, I was instructed to meditate alone in a secluded corner of Domino's yard, while the other coveners prepared the circle. After a lengthy wait, Rhea and Jasmine walked over to me, and signaled it was time to begin. Silently, they walked beside me to the edge of the ritual space where a motionless figure cloaked in black awaited us.

"By what name hast thou chosen to be known as Dedicant of the Coven of the Enchanted Cauldron?" the hooded witch asked me.

"I have chosen the name… Dyffeg," I said proudly.

From beside me, there were muffled sounds.

"What is your name?" the witch asked me again, in a stern voice.

"Dyffeg," I repeated, louder.

There were more noises from Rhea and Jasmine. I could feel their shoulders shaking against mine. Surely, they couldn't be… laughing? Surely not.

After all, this was a very serious ritual.

The witch at the edge of the ritual space then summoned me forward, and the three of us walked into the circle to where the other coveners were waiting.

We stood in front of the altar table.

"Dyffeg, why are you here tonight?" asked one of the witches standing behind the altar.

This time, it was unmistakable. Rhea and Jasmine were giggling, though trying to suppress it. Each time my new witchy name was spoken, it started them all over again. I started laughing as well, as although I wasn't sure of the joke, their laughter was infectious.

We couldn't help ourselves, much to the disgust of a haughty hooded figure I imagined was Judy. All her dire premonitions about my perceived unworthiness were coming to fruition. And that simply made me laugh even more, as much as I tried to stop and adopt a more solemn demeanor in fitting with the occasion.

Afterwards, I found that Rhea (and the other witches) thought I had named myself "the fig" as it sounded like I was saying "de fig."

All she could think was "de apple, de pear, de fig."

Somehow, Jasmine had thought the same thing at the same time.

For a few years afterwards, my nickname in the coven was 'the apple', a play on 'the fig'. Sometimes this was changed to 'the bloody apple,' as an Australian term of affection, or mild exasperation.

Judy was very reserved as we sat around together after the ritual, but most of the other coveners said they thought it was very funny. They declared that it was the most light-hearted Dedication ritual they'd ever attended.

Domino reminded us of the words of the Charge of the Goddess, a beautiful piece of prose (shared by Gerald Gardner) which has a strong influence on contemporary witchcraft practice. Part of 'The Charge' includes the following lines:

"Let my worship be within the heart that rejoiceth, for behold! All acts of love and pleasure are my rituals."

"Our Gods are honored by our happiness as well as by our reverence," Domino said. "We don't have to act self-important and serious all the time. It's OK to have a laugh."

"So mote it be!" Everyone called out and toasted me with glasses of mead as being the first Dedicant of The Coven of the Enchanted Cauldron.

I felt very content. On the plus side of things, being a Dedicant meant that I was entitled to rejoin the 'cool kids' of the Inner Circle of the coven.

Although part of me was sad to spend less time with my new friends the Novices, being involved with running the coven was something I really wanted to experience. I wanted to learn what went on behind the scenes and be involved in the decision-making processes for the coven.

Being a member of the Inner Circle again meant that I was actively involved when lots of interesting changes occurred not long after my Dedication ritual.

A NEW HIGH PRIEST

DOMINO BUMPED INTO CONNOR in the occult book section of the local library. From a pointed conversation, she learnt he was a Wiccan Third Degree High Priest who had undergone his training interstate. His girlfriend relocated back to Queensland to be with her family, and he'd decided to transfer up the East coast to be with her.

Domino immediately seized upon his potential, and impulsively invited him to her house to meet the Inner Circle members of the Coven of the Enchanted Cauldron at our next gathering.

That night, I found myself walking up the stairs behind him, curious about this man with well-fitting jeans. I initially assumed that he was one of the large network of witches from the Golden Sun coven. It wasn't unusual to have seemingly random people join us from time to time, as the local occult community is closely knit.

Connor was in his mid-forties and typified the tall, dark and handsome man spoken of by Gypsy fortune tellers. He spoke passionately and eloquently to us about The Craft and Wicca. He'd trained in a traditional three-degree Wiccan teaching coven, and had then run his own coven for a couple of years.

He was exactly what I had hoped for in a teacher; an experienced practitioner who had gone through a 'proper' coven training to an advanced level.

Most of the Inner Circle were delighted to meet him – Judy a notable exception of course - and after hearing him talk we were keen for him to spend more time with us. Initially he was reluctant to join the coven or take on any leadership position, despite our badgering. He said he needed to take a break, and settle into his new job. But after a lot of begging, he agreed to provide guidance to the coven in a consultancy capacity.

Then, as now, it's rare for a fledgling coven to have the good fortune to find a skilled teacher willing to assist. Most people who wish to create a witch coven learn from a ground-up approach with many lessons from the tried and tested School of Hard Knocks. A knowledgeable witch doesn't usually walk through the door and offer to teach.

I knew that there were dodgy and untrustworthy witches around, including those who charged money for initiation rituals or required sexual favors for advancement, but Connor seemed genuine and knowledgeable.

The introduction of Connor marked a mass exodus of members from the Inner Circle. Judy left in stymied disgust. Another couple of witches found that travelling an hour each way to attend events was becoming too wearying. Three re-joined the Golden Sun coven. Within a month, there were only four Inner Circle members remaining: Domino, Rhea, Jasmine and myself.

During this time, Connor had integrated slowly into the coven. With increased pleading from us, and after considering the reduced number of coven members, he at last agreed to become our High Priest. We four remaining Inner Circle members were delighted about his change of mind.

Over the years, Connor infuriated, challenged and annoyed us, but he also taught, guided and poured his heart out for us. He helped shaped our practices as ritualists and witches, through his exacting high standards. Together, we all reviewed how the coven was working, and put into place some new changes for the future.

Connor was perplexed to learn that we didn't have a coven Book of Shadows, known as a Grimoire or Book of Light and Shadows. He described how Novices in his old coven had to copy by hand certain parts of the Book of Shadows (BoS) during their training. He felt that a Book of Shadows was a vital requirement for a coven, to set out information about the shared rules, rituals, spells and chants. Additionally, it provides structure and continuity for future Novice members.

We set busily to work, creating our own Cauldron of the Enchanted Cauldron Book of Shadows, based on old coven information as well as some snippets from favorite books. Diligently, we used the framework Connor provided to craft our individualized BoS.

Creating our Book of Shadows was like a witchy version of a wedding tradition, with something old (inherited coven tradition); something new (specific to our current practices); something borrowed (thanks, Scott Cunningham and Janet and Stewart Farrar!); and something black instead of blue (the color of the cover).

After we finalized our new coven Book of Shadows, the four Inner Circle members copied the information by hand into our own personal BoS, which we each decorated with pictures, fancy script and images.

I used a recycled ex-government book with a leather spine and corners, which was probably about 40 years old at the time. I loved the smell and sense of age about it, though I wasn't particularly fancy about how I decorated the pages.

Jasmine won the unofficial competition of best decorated BoS by a good length with her beautiful calligraphy, illustrated borders and artwork. Not that it was a competition as such, but she certainly basked in the rosy accolades from Connor while Domino,

Rhea and I subtly rolled our eyes in mild pique at our lesser offerings.

Connor's tradition also harshly dictated that when an initiate resigned from the Coven, their personal BoS was returned to the coven leaders and then burnt. He put this into practice when Scarlet left the coven the following year.

Scarlet was furious about this requirement as she'd spent hours and hours beautifying the pages to create a work of art. She felt that she was being unfairly punished for leaving. Funnily enough, although others eventually left the coven, no more personalized BoS were burnt, so I now agree with Scarlet that the BoS burning was more likely to do with Connor's annoyance with her behavior rather than anything else.

* * *

Connor arranged for the Novices to undergo their Dedication Rite of Passage, so they too could participate in coven rituals. After that, the hard work really began.

We discovered the nit-picking pedant which was hidden inside Connor's amicable persona, particularly when it came to how to perform rituals. He was exacting in his practices, and everyone was required to achieve his very high standards. On every single occasion.

Our rituals contained a lot of words and lines which were spoken while we formed our magical circle space, during the ritual itself, and when ending each ritual. Connor required us to memorize every line and action in advance. Bringing palm-cards or copies of the text into ritual was simply not acceptable. If you stuffed things up, Connor quickly corrected you and his basilisk stare would be felt even on the darkest of nights.

The equipment on the altar had to be arranged in exactly the correct positions. While standing behind the altar, the candle marked with the crescent moon of the Goddess and the chalice containing mead were to the left, where the High Priestess stood. In the middle of the altar were the coven Book of Shadows, the small bowls containing salt, water and oil, and the pentacle on which rested the plate containing cake or biscuits. The bell, incense and the candle marked with the horned symbol of the god was on the side of the High Priest, which was the right side.

"Why does the bell go the right side of the Altar?" we asked him.

"Because the God is always right." Connor responded.

We four women groaned.

We groaned more when we found that the knot which secured the cords we wore around our waist also needed to be worn on the right side. The knot does not go to the middle. Or to the left. Because the God is always right!

The coven adopted a more controlled and ceremonial magic style approach to our rituals, which meant that everyone moved in a certain way (only walk clockwise, never anti clockwise). There was no idle chit chat, frivolity was rare until the more relaxed time of Cakes and Ale when we shared around the chalice of mead, and gestures were precise and deliberate. These gestures included tracing out a pentagram at each of the compass point directions, known as the Quarters.

Woe betides the person who didn't form their movements properly and exactly, as they earned another of Connor's intense stares followed by the quiet instruction to do it again.

This rigorous ritual style seemed quite harsh, but it forced us to change our consciousness away from the everyday, 'shopping list' thoughts, to deliberately focus us on what we are doing, thinking and experiencing while partaking in the shared ritual. We found that when we repeated the memorized actions and words each ritual, it built up a charge of magical resonance between us.

A ritual shared with those who are familiar with all the steps becomes like a flowing and connective dance to faerie music. But that magical resonance took us a lot of time, effort and practice to develop.

INSIDE WITCH RITUALS

A UNIQUE ASPECT OF participating in a witch ritual is energy raising, which is sometimes called creating a Cone of Power. Energy raising involves participants changing their everyday conscious mindset into an almost trance-like state. This helps us to 'see' or feel subtle energy forces or fields. With focused concentration and visualization techniques an energetic charge can be intensified until it is deliberately released or sent to fulfill a specific purpose, such as a magical spell-working or remote healing.

To raise energy and move into a light trance, we coven members learnt to use music, chanting, drumming and dance or movement as techniques. Raising energy effectively in a group is both a skill and an art, as it takes practice as well as a sense of altered awareness.

We always used energy raising techniques during Esbats (full moon rituals), when the High Priestess – or woman in that role - performed Drawing Down the Moon. Drawing Down involves invoking the spirit of the Goddess through ecstatic channeling or trance. Connor taught we four women of the Inner Circle techniques to do this and instructed us to meditate every day.

During the process of invocation, the Priestess becomes the embodiment of a pre-Christian Goddess. The woman becomes 'more' than herself, and often receives great insights and visions as she personifies the divine within us all.

The face, shape and voice of the Priestess can completely change during the process of invocation, occasionally with an enormous aura of light around her body. Other peculiar things can occur. For example, when Rhea invoked the Goddess, her body used to rock forwards and backwards, like a pendulum. She would tilt and sway by almost 45 degrees. We would hold our breath, semi-terrified that she would fall over, but she never has.

Experiencing a Drawing Down can have quite a profound impact on those witnessing it, and it's not uncommon for people to weep or feel a range of intense emotions. It seems like the Divine Spirit is talking directly to you with a meaningful and personalized message, which resonates on many levels.

In accordance with our longstanding coven practices, the Priestess recites a modified version of The Charge of the Goddess during the process of Drawing Down the Moon. The Charge of Goddess is a series of lovely poetic verses compiled by Gerald Gardner and influenced by a range of occultists and historical writings. Before Drawing Down occurred, all the TEC witches except the High Priestess and High Priest would raise energy by singing the Witches Rune (popularized by Doreen Valiente and Gerald Gardner) multiple times while we danced around the circle.

As we ran and chanted, the Inner Circle member in the High Priestess role stood in the center of the ritual space, with Connor kneeling before her. She focused on assuming a trance state until the culmination and release of our energy raising.

This same method of dancing and chanting was used in the old Golden Sun coven, as well as by Connor's previous coven. Usually we sang the whole Witches Rune chant through at least three times while first walking, then dancing then finally running around the circle. We were very fit witches!

Singing the Witches Rune wasn't well liked by a few of us. Rhea and some of the other members would mutter darkly about needing to chant what felt like a million verses while dancing rhythmically around the circle:

"Do we HAVE to do The Witches Rune? Can't we just chant something shorter?"

"Bloody Witches Rune. Bloody hate it."

"I keep getting all the verses mixed up. Can't we just use the chorus? It's too looOOOoong!"

"We used to do it in my old coven. We will do it in this coven." That was Connor's response.

Even twenty plus years later, I still recall the first time the Coven of The Enchanted Cauldron chanted the Witches Rune with Connor as High Priest. Connor was kneeling in front of Jasmine, who was lucky to be chosen as the first covener to undertake Drawing Down.

We began our intoning the Rune while walking around the periphery of the circle.

Suddenly Connor stood up and berated us all.

"I have never seen such a pathetic attempt at energy raising in my entire life! Do it again!"

If he'd been a cartoon figure there would have been steam coming out of his ears. He knelt again and off we set, drumming and chanting the Witches Rune from the beginning until:

Connor: "No, NO! Move together! Step together!"

Coveners: "Darksome night and shin-"

Connor: "And beat that goddamn drum in a regular beat."

Coveners (again): "Darksome night and shining moon..."

Connor: "No, no, NO! Keep your distance. Don't group up. Look at yourselves - five of you are on top of each other, and the other three are right around the other side of the circle!"

Finally, he gave up trying to instruct us from the center of the circle, and made each of us grab hold of the cord which was tied around the waist of the witch in front of us. We then had to move like synchronized swimmers marching in exact order with the other witches in the circle, while he beat the drum. It felt like we were in a bloody army. Left foot, right foot, left foot, right foot.

Around and around the circle we marched. Eventually we were able to keep in perfect rhythm and tempo with the drum beat as it altered our pace from fast to slow. We must have looked like strange automatons to a casual observer.

Then Scarlet, as she is never successful at repressing strong emotions, made the mistake of complaining about how difficult it was to beat the drum, chant and run at the same time.

"It's okay for you to stand there and beat the drum, Connor. You aren't the one running around the bloody circle!" she said.

In response to her comment we were then treated to the sight of Connor almost flying around the circle, dark hair streaming out behind him as he ran in a smooth and unperturbed manner, beating the drum in perfect rhythm. The best way to describe his motion is to compare him to a graceful Elf in a Lord of the Rings movie, moving effortlessly over the snow.

His demonstration silenced all of us, and we knew that this high standard was what we needed to aspire to. When Connor finished three renditions of the Witches Rune he was hardly breathless. Our complaints were effectively silenced.

From that very practical experience we learnt to keep in time with the drum and maintain equal space between each other while creating a Cone of Power. We also learnt that effective energy raising involves a sensation of pushing the energy or 'chi' forward, towards the witch ahead of you. When everyone does this pushing sensation, the energy circulates freely among the group. Done properly, energy raising creates a wonderful feeling of connection and vitality, and to the psychically attuned eye, you can see a white/ pale blue electric-style current whizz around the circle.

The final aspect of energy raising is learning when and how to release it. There is definitely a 'sweet spot' associated with timing the release of the focused energy-charge. If the group releases the energy too soon it is not as effective, and if you continue past the energy-wave peak, the flow falters. The latter mistake is very easily identified by tired witches staggering wearily around the circle, chanting with hoarse, cracking voices.

At the (hopefully) optimal time, one of the witches cries out "DOWN" when they feel the group energy is at its strongest. This signal is the cue for the participating witches to release or send the energy-charge in the pre-determined direction.

After releasing energy we immediately lower ourselves to a sitting or lying position on the ground, which allows any excess energy to be released and gives us a well-earned rest. It also allows a quiet time for reflection and enables any personal visions or insights to be received. Lying on the ground surrounded by companion witches and gazing into the night skies can be one of the best aspects of ritual.

FIRST DEGREE INITIATIONS

AFTER MENTORING US to a satisfactory level of ritual experience, Connor's next goal was for Rhea, Jasmine, Domino and I to complete our First Degree Initiation.

In the Wiccan Initiation framework that Connor was familiar with, which had three levels or Degrees to be attained, each Degree has certain requirements coveners need to achieve prior to the initiation ceremony. While it's not compulsory to undergo any kind of initiation to be a witch, a Degree system is quite satisfying as it sets clear goals to guide learning.

The is no one standardized witchy Degree system, and while there can be similarities between coven systems there may be significant differences. It comes down to the tradition or style of working followed by the coven, which can vary radically, depending on the shared gnosis of the members or the desires of the leader.

Within our current coven system, the Dedication ritual is the first of four Rites of Passage, followed consecutively by First, Second and lastly Third Degree Initiation. The timing of the Dedication ritual can vary from six weeks to more than a year after the Novice joins the coven. For First, Second and Third Initiations, there is at least a year – often multiple years – between each, to allow time for the assimilation of learning.

Connor explained that First Degree Initiates need to demonstrate they had foundational witchcraft knowledge and some aptitude in divination. We would be tested on these by undergoing a written test and by performing a psychic divination reading. The sting in the tail was that we required a 95% pass mark in the written exam.

How conscientiously the four of us studied for our First Degree Initiation exam: herbs, crystals, history, magical correspondences, alphabets in other languages, the Eightfold Wheel of the Year, Astrology and anything else we could think of. We tested each other, and filled notebooks with esoteric scribbles.

On the day of the exam I arrived at Connor's house, almost bursting with pent up knowledge.

However, only three of the four Inner Circle members - Rhea, Jasmine and myself - turned up. We waited, but Domino didn't arrive. Nor did she answer her home phone when Connor tried to contact her.

We were puzzled by her non-appearance. Repeated phone calls to her brought no response, and we then became worried that something had gone wrong, or she'd had an accident.

Finally, as there was nothing else we could do, the three of us worked our way through our examination papers, and with a feeling of completion, handed them to Connor. After a nail-biting wait while he marked our tests, we received happy news: We had all passed!

A few days later, Rhea, Jasmine and I finally discovered what had happened to the mysteriously missing Domino, who didn't turn up for her First Degree Initiation test.

We three met again at Connor's house, surrounded in the usual fog of cigarette smoke, with me sitting slightly back to minimize my passive smoking exposure.

Connor explained that Domino had at last returned his phone calls and explained why she didn't arrive on the day of the exam.

"She didn't need to do the exam, because she is already a Third Degree witch." Connor leaned back in his chair, took a drag on his cigarette and waited expectantly for our reactions. He wasn't disappointed.

We were dumbfounded. Domino had previously only completed her Dedication Ritual, the same as we other women. She certainly wasn't a Third Degree Initiate as far as we knew. Amidst howls of disbelief, we begged Connor for further information.

"Domino told me that she has been doing witchcraft for years and running the coven. She said she didn't need to be tested. She believes she already is the equivalent of a Third Degree and didn't need a take an exam to prove it."

He went on to explain that Domino had said that she didn't need Connor, she didn't need us, no one was going to tell her what to do, and she was going to run her own new coven. With her as Third Degree High Priestess. Please don't contact her again, because she didn't trust any of us.

Wow. Impressive. A lot.

I would learn over the years that this kind of erratic - and sometimes extreme - behavior was potentially part of the Initiation journey for some people. The lead-up to Initiation can be a highly emotional, as we spend time deliberately reflecting on our life's journey, achievements and inner being. This process includes – or should include - a lot of self-questioning and reviewing the life-choices that led to our current situation. In response to this focused introspection, the psyche can often respond in alarming or upsetting ways.

Initiation preparation is not only an internal process, as witches can also experience significant and unexpected changes in their external life circumstances, either prior to Initiation or not long afterwards. Sometimes it seems that the Gods (or our own Higher Self) like to test us on all levels, and grind us through the mill of life's difficulties as part of Initiation preparations.

Transformation is a key aspect of what we do as witches, but that doesn't mean that all transformations are easy or joyful. Some transformations can be difficult and painful, for the individual themselves as well as for the people around them. Like a snake shedding its skin, the outer casing becomes tight, itchy and uncomfortable before it is cast off to reveal the beautiful patterns and scales beneath. And then in time this too is shed to reveal the new skin.

Connor described Domino's actions as an 'ego explosion.' He'd seen this occur before, sometimes just as a mild tantrum which calmed after a hug, soothing conversation and a good night's sleep. At the other end of the spectrum, it could include a complete personality-change at Drama-Queen meltdown level. Domino's reaction was definitely at the more extreme end of the spectrum.

He postulated that she was terrified of failing the examination and losing face, so instead she decided that she was so far in advance that she didn't require any kind of test. And we, who had been her friends, were sadly now her foes.

It was a sobering discussion, and I grieved at the loss of our previous friendship. We had shared so many good times together, and it seemed strange and hurtful that she no longer wanted to be a member of our coven.

I never saw Domino again. Apparently, she started to wear a red cord in public rituals as a sign of her self-avowed Third Degree status. Rumor has it that the High Priest of the Golden Sun coven was slightly irked by that, and in response decided to switch the entire cord color association of the coven around, so that a red cord was the mark of the lowliest new recruit rather than of the highest grade.

Also, apparently, she broke up with her long-term partner, and found true love with a wealthy older man. Rumor also has it that when Domino moved out of our old covenstead, there was a room-sized pile of rotting clothes on the floor of the carport which had to be power-hosed out of the concrete. Where she is now, I do not know, but I hope she is happy.

*** * * ***

Connor, with the assistance of a local High Priestess who'd been initiated in Avalon (Glastonbury in England), initiated Rhea, Jasmine and me to First Degree on the same night. The white cords of a Novice, which we wore tied around our waists over our robes, were exchanged for the yellow cords of a First Degree initiate.

Even more excitingly, we were now entitled to wear an athame, which is a black handled, double edged knife, sheathed on our cords. In our tradition, the athame is a symbol of authority and is never used to cut anything physical or alive.

It was a deeply significant, life changing and special ritual.

Although I took vows not to discuss what occurred during the ritual, one defining aspect of the initiation that I can talk about is that we Initiates needed to be completely naked, or sky clad, during the ritual. This prerequisite included not wearing any clothes while we walked from where we meditated in solitude, down to the edge of the ritual space.

The reason for this state of undress is that Initiations are perceived as new beginnings, or births. As we are born into this world as naked infants, First Degree Initiation marks a new birth, or a second beginning into our mundane as well as spiritual lives.

Jasmine even had to remove her body piercings to comply with this requirement.

I know that being sky-clad in a ritual can be very confronting. It forces us up against our feelings of disgust related to what we think is less than perfect or attractive with our bodies. Boobs too saggy, tummy too soft, thighs too large, tuck-shop-lady arms, too old. All those stupid, superficial fears emerge with the threat of exposing our secret skin to others.

And that's one of the reasons that we perform certain rituals with no clothing; to work through those anxieties. Removing our clothing to reveal our bodies beneath, in a setting of trust, respect and reverence is very healing. Because every person is beautiful and glorious in their own skin. When the masking clothes are removed, it reminds us that there is no such thing as a 'perfect' or 'ideal' body... we are all human in our own inimitable style.

On the night of my First Degree Initiation, when I cast off the covering blanket which protected me from the biting mosquitos, and stood up naked in the night, I felt glorious. I felt like an ancient pagan Goddess walking through the land, with flowers springing up in my footprints. There were no feelings of shame, or trepidation. I was proud of my strong body and knew that I was in exactly the place and space I needed to be.

CELEBRATING THE WHEEL OF THE YEAR

A FEW MONTHS LATER I was privileged to officiate as High Priestess at the First Degree Initiations for Meredith and Scarlet. It was a great experience to be on the other side of the initiatory experience and welcome our new First Degree witches into the coven.

As well as initiations, the coven continued to celebrate with shared rituals each full moon (called Esbats) and seasonal turning points (called Sabbats). I like how these rituals each have their own different meaning and significance.

Esbats are private and intimate rituals which include Drawing Down the Moon and energy raising using the nefarious Witches Rune chant. These rituals were strictly for coveners only.

The Sabbats are celebrated at each solstice, equinox and at equidistant times in-between. Collectively, the eight Sabbats are referred to as the Wheel of the Year. These ceremonies remind us to participate fully in seasonal changes, which are experienced externally in nature as well as internally within our psyche. By celebrating the changing seasons, we also activate our internal cycles for personal growth and development.

Australian pagans experience challenges with the Northern Hemisphere Wheel of the Year system, as our seasons are different from those of our European spiritual kin. Books written in England or North America need to be re-interpreted to our local country, as it defies logic why we witches should be celebrating the warmth of summer solstice in the middle of winter!

Our coven celebrates the eight Sabbat rituals by changing our ritual themes to correspond with what is occurring seasonally in the Australian landscape around us. This means that we celebrate at the opposite seasons to Northern Hemisphere pagans, as we place the winter solstice (Yule) in July and the summer solstice (Litha) in December. Our Autumn Equinox is celebrated close to Easter time and Spring Equinox occurs just in time for the school holidays.

Therefore, Samhuin, the Celtic fire festival which is similar to Halloween, is celebrated at the end of April. This Southern Hemisphere change has local synchronicities, as this time when we witches honor our ancestors aligns with ANZAC day commemorations which acknowledge the sacrifices of those who have gone before us.

Imbolc, Beltane and Lughnasadh are the other three Celtic fire festivals which complete the Wheel of the Year. Imbolc, which is when we celebrate the promise of spring with nine lit candles, occurs in early August. This is one of my favorite Sabbats, as it focuses on the Celtic Goddess Brigit, who is patron of poetry, smith-craft and healing. Brigit is a special being, as she is regarded as a historical personage as well as a Saint in the Catholic religion.

We refer to Beltane as the 'lusty' Sabbat. It has the opposite emphasis to Samhuin. While Samhuin focuses on death, the ancestors and the Other-worlds, Beltane honors sex, joy, lust and fertility. In Australia, the days at the end of October are warm – but without the full heat of summer - and the Earth is languid and fruitful.

The harvest festival of Lughnasadh is celebrated around the beginning of February in Australia. This Sabbat reminds us to acknowledge what we have reaped from the previous year and to plan our spiritual and personal goals for the next year.

Each of our Sabbat rituals include a dramatic re-enactment of pre-Christian myth-stories that link to these pivotal times of the year. The ceremonies are deliberately performance-like, and very enjoyable. There is a lovely contrast between the more reverent Esbat rituals and the relaxed and sociable Sabbat celebrations.

Now that our coven had some decent ritual experience under our colored cords, we decided to invite members of the 'general public' to a couple of our Sabbat rituals. As Rhea had experience in event management, Meredith had organizing expertise, Scarlet had a lot of flair in general and I loved to get my teeth into anything, we designed our first public ritual under Connor's watchful eyes.

We were ruthless in our preparations. Each covener was rostered for a range of duties, such as welcoming new people or picking up cigarette butts. We practiced extensively to ensure our ritual had symbolic meaning and was aesthetically enjoyable. Finally, we photocopied flyers to place in bookshops and local letterboxes, on public noticeboards and under the windscreen wipers of cars. It was the 1990's version of internet spamming!

Our only concern was that although we were on the private property of our friendly Avalonian Priestess friend, what we were doing was illegal. Yes, in accordance with our local laws, we were criminals.

Queensland's Criminal Code included a section called 'Pretending to Exercise Witchcraft or Tell Fortunes' which threatened imprisonment with one year's hard labor for the following offences:

Pretended to one to exercise [or use] witchcraft [or sorcery or enchantment or conjuration].

Undertook to one to tell his [or her] future fortunes.

Pretended to one, by virtue of a pretended skill in [or knowledge of] some occult science, to discover where [or in what manner] certain goods supposed to have been stolen [or lost] might be found.

(Section 432 Queensland Criminal Code 1899)

This law was only repealed in the year 2000. Prior to that, we would joke by saying that as we weren't 'pretending' to practice witchcraft and really 'were' practicing witchcraft we weren't doing anything illegal. Or so we hoped, anyways. We knew that we were taking a risk by promoting our Sabbat ritual so widely, but we were young and brave. And we were not pretending at all.

No police turned up to our first ritual to imprison us to a year's hard labor. Instead seventy people arrived to join in with our Beltane celebrations!

Beltane is the sexy Sabbat, celebrating fertility and joyous unions. Our ritual focused around the death of the Sun King, and how He was returned to life by the yearning call of the Goddess, so they could celebrate this abundant time of year together.

In accordance with this theme, the covener who took on the role of the King symbolically 'died' in the middle of the ritual space and his 'corpse' was covered over with a richly patterned cloak. This signaled a time of mourning for the ceremony's participants, so seventy people shrieked and moaned in dramatized sorrow.

After a short time of mourning, I declaimed aloud the beautifully crafted words, featured in Gardner's Witchcraft Today book which began with:

"Queen of the Moon. Queen of the Sun. Darkness and tears are set aside when the sun shall come up early."

Then, with a bit of prompting, all participants began chanting in unison: "Bring back the King! Bring back the King! Bring back the King!"

This was the signal for our three gorgeously attired belly dancers - Scarlet, Deirdre and Jasmine - to dance around the circle to the evocative rhythm of a Loreena McKennit song.

Finally, our fallen King could no longer resist the enticements of the beckoning dancers. Connor, in the guise of the King, cast off his covering cloak, jumped to his feet and cried: "I am reborn!"

Everyone cheered and clapped, rejoicing in the return of the Beltane King. To celebrate, we shared spiced mead and honey cakes. At the end of the ritual everyone feasted on delicious food and drank the remnants of the mead until late into the night.

Basking in the success of our public Beltane ritual, we next planned a public Litha ritual. This was held at the height of an Australian summer. The ceremony featured coveners dressed as the Oak King and the Holly King, battling for supremacy at the time of the summer solstice.

The two opposing Kings slashed at each other with metal swords, which made wonderful clanging noises as the blades met, until the symbolic death of the Oak King occurred. Thankfully, no coveners were harmed in the process, though many wonderful memories were created.

GROWING A COVEN

GLOWING WITH THE SUCCESS of our public rituals, The Coven of the Enchanted Cauldron advertised for new Novices to join us. Ten months later, this intake was followed by even more new witches. Our coven numbered about twenty members, despite some witches leaving for a variety of reasons, including changes in work hours or being asked to resign due to erratic behavior. During this time, we three women of the Inner Circle continued to learn about the practicalities of running a large coven while rotating through the High Priestess role.

When the whole coven was together we were a large and noisy group. As Jasmine didn't possess enough chairs in her house to seat us all, everyone was asked to bring their own chair to lessons. We also created the sensible practice of starting a beverage list, which included each covener's preference for tea, coffee, hot chocolate or herbal drinks, as well as milk, sugar or honey requirements. To support this list, we also created a tea-making roster, to prevent fifteen plus people hovering around the urn at one time.

Incidentally, on the practical side of things, purchasing an urn is a sound investment for those times when a big cackle of witches gathers. We love our tea and coffee!

I found that growing a coven, Novice intake by Novice intake – or new member by new member - isn't all a bed of soft and fragrant rose petals. There are spikey thorns involved, as well as the sweet perfume of positive experiences.

One lesson I learnt through the School of Hard Knocks is the importance of being selective when choosing who will join your coven. Although some people label witch covens as being like a cult, in fact they are the opposite. A reputable coven is quite difficult to join due to rigorous screening processes but is easy to leave when members wish to do so. And that is exactly how it should be.

Our screening processes included reading the person's written application and then conducting a face-to-face interview if they seemed reasonable on paper. On the application form, we asked them to describe why they wished to join the coven, what experience they'd had previously, and to describe their strengths and weaknesses when working in a group. In many ways, this process is similar to applying for any new job.

We interviewed a large range of people who wished to join the coven. Pagans and witches are generally inclusive and forgiving folk. We genuinely want to embrace the best in people and usually focus on the beauty within others, rather than the perhaps less-than-perfect surface or superficial traits. Society's outcasts, misfits, mystics and dreamers may find a seat by the pagan's hearth. But for group dynamics, we tried to be careful in choosing who would be sitting around the coven fire with us.

I discovered some of the peculiar reasons people wished to join a coven. For example:

Applicant: "I want to learn how to curse my ex-partner."
Me: *Oops, no, sorry. Wanting to join a coven so you can learn how to harm someone is not an appropriate reason. Seeking professional remedial counseling would be a better choice.*

Applicant: "I have spent 1000 soul lifetimes in contact with you through different reincarnations and I know this is my destiny."

Me: *That's very flattering to hear, thank you. But this one occasion in this lifetime is quite enough, and I'm going to keep it that way.*

Applicant: "My boyfriend has joined a gym, and I've got nothing to do in the evenings."
Me: *Please don't join a coven because you are lonely, or to 'get back at' someone that you have a grudge against. These are not great reasons.*

Applicant: "Because I look frick'n fantastic wearing black clothing, silver jewelry and heavy mascara. And I've got the best hardcore tattoos ever."
Me: *Indeed, you do. You look awesome! I feel so boring and 'soccer mum' in what I'm wearing right now. I don't even have a tattoo. However, unless there is some substance and deep connections behind such superficiality, it's unlikely to be a long-term relationship.*

Despite our screening process, we made some terrible mistakes, including accepting a pedophile, a couple of charming sociopaths and a compulsive liar. While we intuitively felt something wasn't quite right with some applicants, we wanted to give them a chance to blossom into their own star-beauty within the coven.

Some personality traits simply cause too many interpersonal issues, and having a probationary system is handy when group dynamics didn't work out. Some new Novices didn't even last out the probation period, particularly if they didn't complete the homework activities in the set timeframe.

On the other hand, we also found a lot of people who immediately 'clicked' with our coven. We instinctively knew that they were future members of our exclusive company of witches. These are the people who you can call in the middle of the night, in the crazy shipwreck times of life, and they will be there for you. As you are there for them when they need it. That's part of the emotional, intellectual and magical links between coveners.

As we interviewed the applicants, we learnt of the concept of egregore. In simple terms, egregore is the invisible soul or spirit of a group. When the group's egregore is strong, members feel connected into the same vibration. You feel like you are part of something bigger than yourself... and you are. Inspiration flows between members and there is mutual love and respect for everyone in a group which has strong egregore. People who don't fit the group egregore either won't join or won't stay if the egregore is not appropriate for them.

Conversely, a weak or fragmented egregore will lead to fluxes in membership, poor relationships between members and psychologically destructive events.

Egregore is a two-way process. Members effect the egregore of the group and the egregore effects the members of the group. This certainly isn't group-think or a brainwashing situation, despite the synchronicities which occur in a closely-knit coven (such as when everyone turns up wearing the same color clothing). After all, witches are an individualistic mob of people, and proud to be that way.

SECOND DEGREE, SHADOW WORK AND MORE CHANGES

LIKE ANY ORGANIC SUBSTANCE, covens go through cycles of growth, stability, collapse and regrowth. After a few vibrant years of growth and new experiences, The Coven of the Enchanted Cauldron's phase of decay insidiously began by the end of the 1990s.

One destructive tendril grew an ugly green shade of jealousy among a couple of new female coveners, because of the actions of one of our very attractive male witches. Luke had been in a different coven before joining TEC and brought with him a philosophy cherishing the joy of sex and advanced flirtation techniques.

Most pagans and witches believe that sex is natural and wonderful, something to be celebrated rather than shunned, so there were no issues there. Unfortunately, two of the female Novices found Luke's sexy charisma irresistible, much to his delight.

One thing led to another, and he finally became intimate with one of his admirers in the late hours of the night after a ritual. This act blew the lid off a bubbling pot of discontentment and jealousy, when the other covener found out about it. She believed that she was the worthier recipient of Luke's attention, and that the two of them were soul-kin. She was devastated that he'd slept with her competitor for his affections.

To complicate things, the so called 'lucky woman' became emotionally distraught after the physical act, as she found it wasn't a prelude to an ongoing relationship, as she had hoped. She had told her existing boyfriend that she was leaving him, only to find that the male covener considered that night to be a one-off fling between consenting adults.

Hell hath no fury like a woman scorned, and here we had at least two of them in our coven, with the man in question blithely unaware of the repercussions from that night of passion.

While no touchy-feely-sex stuff happened in ritual or lessons, and in general the coven felt like a safe space, interpersonal dynamics became very troubled. Like any grand television drama, there were frosty stares, emotional whispering and teary communications in corners of the covenstead. The telephone lines burnt hot with gossip and accusations. We changed from a happy, respectful group to one experiencing the worse kind of high-school, teenage angst. Somehow, everyone knew exactly what had transpired, and there were at least three versions of the story.

From a coven leader perspective, the situation was a total mess. There were a lot of conversations featuring sodden tissues, and angry outbursts which were sympathized-with and soothed. Somehow, eventually, the relationships were salvaged, with the result being that the two females become firm friends through their shared experience of rejection. The male covener finally recognized the need to keep his distance when it came to potentially troublesome relationships with other coveners.

✳ ✳ ✳

The work of the coven continued. The Wheel of the Year's seasons and phases of the moon were celebrated in ritual. And the date of Second Degree Initiation for Rhea, Jasmine and me finally arrived.

Second Degree Initiation preparations were quite an intense time for the three of us. Through meditation, one's life is considered under fine scrutiny to sort the dross from the gold. Those habits or practices which no longer serve us are acknowledged and released. This initiation requires a deeper examination of the psyche, and involves what we call Shadow Work.

Concepts of the Shadow come from Jungian psychology and relate to the often-negative aspects of the personality of which we are usually not consciously aware. Carl Jung (1938) believed that everyone "...*carries a shadow, and the less it is embodied in the individual's conscious life, the blacker and denser it is.*"

Shadow Work involves the difficult and demanding process of becoming aware of your own Shadow, interacting with it and ultimately assimilating with it. This is difficult for a few reasons, particularly because we can't easily identify our own Shadow-self as it is usually hidden from our conscious awareness.

We deliberately bury our Shadow-self and prefer not to acknowledge the existence of it, despite being clearly able to see similar negative traits (for example jealousy, lying, laziness) in others. The main reason we do this is because gazing upon our Shadow-selves is usually an emotionally harrowing experience, as we don't like what we see, or it causes us emotional pain.

The process of Shadow Work can be undertaken in a variety of ways, including dream analysis, meditation workings, diligent self-reflection and journaling. Having very honest and loving friends who are able to provide helpful feedback – which can sometimes make us feel brutally raw – is also extremely useful to assist us to understand our own Shadow-self. Of course, the challenge here is that everyone's perspectives are slightly (or majorly!) skewed to some degree by their own Shadow-self.

Shadow Work is not a quick process. Integration is a lifelong journey, and we are all at different stages along our individual paths. One shortcut I've found useful in the quest of discovering one's Shadow-self, is to become aware of your interactions with other people. Are there people in your life who you really dislike, or don't 'get?' Do certain people have personality traits that irk you, or make you angry? Look again, closer this time. Often, these are components of your own Shadow-self that you are seeing reflected back at you by the actions of other people. This can be a valuable lesson, although initially we may not like what we see.

I believe Shadow Work is hard but very necessary work, as magic, the psyche and spirituality are integrally linked. Perhaps this is why witchcraft is not for everyone, as not all of us have the driving will and desire to deliberately do the tough work of finding and working with our Shadow-self so that it is no longer a hidden and terrifying monster.

Sometimes Shadow Work is done deliberately, but at other times the greater guiding influence of the 'Universe' will demand that we wake up and see our true selves clearly. Due to sudden and unexpected life changes, we are jolted off the comfortable railway tracks of our lives, and moved sideways onto a different track of self-awareness.

An increase in the frequency of meditation sessions and Shadow Work certainly jolted me off my seemingly pre-determined life-railway-tracks, while preparing for Second Degree. Major changes included a huge relationship shake up and moving to a new house. But there were a lot of positives for me during that time, and by the night of Second Degree Initiation I was ready physically, mentally, spiritually and emotionally.

Once again, Rhea, Jasmine and I did our Initiations together, completing Second Degree in December 1997 in our beautiful circle close by to the bay. It was an amazing and visionary night, and the four of us celebrated this significant milestone well into the wee hours, with drinks and food around the fire. We each bought the same little pewter witch statue as a tangible reminder of the night, and my statue still shares space on my altar.

It was wonderful to exchange the yellow cord of a First Degree initiate for the blue cord of Second Degree witch. We wore these with pride around our waists during ritual and delighted in our new title of 'Lady.'

Although we were given the option to change our magical witch names within the ritual, I chose to keep my unique name of Dyffeg. I was now 'Lady Dyffeg.' And given the study and work that needed to be achieved before this Initiation, I certainly felt I'd earned this new title.

More coven-change tendrils grew from the Second Degree Initiation. A few days afterwards, I received a clear insight that I should not commence the curriculum leading towards Third Degree Initiation, which was our pre-determined pathway. I knew at a deeper level that Third Degree was not the right course for me to take, despite the disappointment of Rhea and Jasmine when I let them know. They were surprised and found my decision difficult to understand.

The threads of our threefold witchy-woman Inner Circle partnership began to slowly unravel.

With this change in the balance of coven leadership, Connor then broached the topic of moving to a more 'traditional' model of having one High Priestess and High Priest to run the coven. This is the system that he'd trained with, and the norm for Wiccan covens at that time.

The three of us women had really enjoyed our previous rotational High Priestess role, however now it was down to just Rhea and Jasmine, as only they were studying towards Third Degree Initiation. But all three of us women thought that it would be good to experience a 'traditional' structure, so we agreed to this change.

The decision to choose either Rhea or Jasmine as TEC High Priestess had big implications for the coven's future. Jasmine was a physically beautiful, warm, easygoing woman with a lovely laugh. She and Connor got on like a house on fire. On the other hand, Rhea was of more generous proportions and tended to challenge or question Connor at times, which he never enjoyed. But she lived and breathed witchcraft from the depths of her soul, and is incredibly intelligent, gregarious and generous.

Connor chose Jasmine as the High Priestess of the coven.

In some ways, I felt it was a contest between a gentle feminine persona (Jasmine) and not as conventionally girly (Rhea). I will admit to bias in this situation, as I have a close friendship with Rhea, forged during the time of my expulsion from the Inner Circle. Nevertheless, I still thought that Rhea would make a far better High Priestess for our coven.

Despite my personal preferences, Jasmine did a gracious job as High Priestess, and Connor continued to whole heartedly support Rhea towards her Third Degree Initiation. I assisted in running the Novice training programs, and we still were meeting once or twice a week as a coven, so things were ticking along quite smoothly on the surface. I attended some of the Third Degree preparation lessons as well, so that was enjoyable learning too.

However, things just weren't the same anymore.

COVEN RE-BOOT

THERE WERE MORE CHANGES. It wasn't just one thing; it was little snowballs that turned into a gliding avalanche. Perhaps some of us didn't like the newest Novices as much as we did the existing members. I certainly didn't feel as engaged because I wasn't as intrinsically involved in running the coven as I had been previously.

The coven grew larger and larger with multiple Novice intakes, and distinct 'camps' developed. A coven is as much about relationships between members as it is about anything else, and things didn't seem to harmonize like they used to. Something in the Coven of the Enchanted Cauldron just seemed to be missing for me.

Rhea continued to put everything she had into her Third Degree preparations, and a year and a day after Second Degree she was elevated to the Third Degree. After sharing First and Second Degree Initiations with Jasmine and I, she was the only one of the three of us who made it through to the ultimate Wiccan Degree. I was very proud of her achievement.

Despite being appointed High Priestess of the coven, Jasmine didn't complete her own Third Degree Initiation. Instead, she was delighted to become pregnant with a second (and unexpected) child during her studies. Sadly, it was a difficult pregnancy, and she needed to spend a lot of time resting. Due to health and family demands, Jasmine started to spend more time away from the coven. As Rhea and I didn't have children of our own, we gradually grew more distant from her as Jasmine's focus moved to her growing family.

About that time, Connor decided he would like to create a new coven, in his own specific lineage and tradition. The Coven of the Enchanted Cauldron naturally divided into two main groups. It was a very amicable split. Those coveners who wished to join with Connor did so, and those who wished to continue with Rhea and The Coven of the Enchanted Cauldron were invited to do so.

Other coveners decided on completely different options, including joining the local women-only coven, studying with friends or simply getting on with various other aspects of life's journey.

When Rhea assumed the mantle of High Priestess of the Coven of the Enchanted Cauldron, she asked me to be Coven Maiden, and I gladly accepted. Coven Maiden is the right-hand-woman of the High Priestess, and is responsible for getting things done and ensuring ritual equipment and supplies were in good working order. It is a prestigious role, and I certainly was very happy to help out.

Meredith and Scarlet also continued with Rhea. They were both glad of the change, Scarlet in particular. Too many times she'd been criticized by Connor, with her witchy conduct perceived as lacking. I'd lost count of the number of times her athame fell off her cord, only to be found by Connor on the ritual ground and returned to her with a raising of the eyebrows. She was also renowned at getting her lines slightly mixed up, earning her a frustrated sigh.

Informally, we called The Coven of the Enchanted Cauldron re-boot under Rhea's leadership TEC two (TEC2), to differentiate between the coven under Connor's stewardship and the new structure. Rhea brought in many excellent changes and a burst of new energy. Our covenstead moved to Rhea's house and our circle for rituals was hosted on Scarlet's five-acre property, both West of the city. We become more grounded in ancient Celtic mythology, changing our circle set-up and ritual focus accordingly.

Over a couple of years, we experienced many great times together as TEC2. We brought in new Novices and elevated a High Priest. We performed some exceptional rituals, such as the one where we crafted a five-meter-long tube of black fabric to mimic an adult-sized vagina and crawled through it during the ritual. One quite rotund member got stuck, but we managed to midwife him out the other end. During other rituals, we killed the Corn King at Mabon, and banished winter and welcomed spring at Imbolc.

But I still felt the need for a change. I wanted to spread my magical wings wider and have greater autonomy. Finally, I resigned from the Coven of the Enchanted Cauldron.

THE POWER OF THREE: A NEW COVEN

RESIGNING FROM TEC 2 was the right decision to make. I found that I didn't like the new High Priest much, despite enjoying his company initially. Rhea was extremely confident in her role, and no longer needed me to support her as Coven Maiden. The coven rituals no longer inspired me, and I felt like I was doing the same thing over and over, so it was definitely time for me to leave.

On a couple of occasions, I met with Scarlet and Meredith for a chat. Meredith let us know that she was having difficulties at work, and she'd appreciate some additional magical support. This led to us performing spell craft together, to improve the situation. I was awed at the sense of spontaneity and creativity that flowed when I was together with these two other witches. Rituals felt enjoyable again.

Eventually, Scarlet and Meredith resigned from TEC2, and we created an informal affiliation. During this time, Rhea, our previous High Priestess, continued to train witches in the TEC style for a few more years. Later, she became an initiate in Traditional Witchcraft and continues to be our dear friend. We often all catch up for a Thai meal and birthday celebrations together.

Scarlet, Meredith and I joyfully moved away from a rigid coven structure, from which we had learnt so much, into something that was incredibly freeform. We delighted in the differences: for example, we could laugh and ad-lib in ritual as there was no leader tapping us on the shoulder, or junior witches for whom we needed to be an example. We could make up lines. We could do weird stuff. We could primal scream. There were no Novices to train, or boss-witches to chastise us for dropping our athame.

It was FUN!!!!

We performed our rituals on Scarlet's property, in her private ritual space close by the chicken pen. Yes, I admit there were a few jokes made about having potential sacrifices (the hens) so handy to our ritual area. But no chickens were ever harmed, though they might have been slightly sleep-deprived by some of our loud chanting. Our circle was guarded by a statue of Pan, and ha a variety of herbs growing around the edge of it.

Like teenagers new to uncontrolled freedom, we rebelled against a few practices from The Coven of the Enchanted Cauldron. What was particularly satisfying was ruthlessly paring back all our coven equipment so that our needs could be carried in one small box. This meant that there were no more trips to the far reaches of the paddock with a bulky suitcase on wheels, an iron cauldron, a massive sword, extra ritual equipment 'just in case,' as well as food and drinks. We loved minimalizing our ritual tool requirements!

Our new altar was an old tree stump in the South of our ritual circle, so we didn't need to carry a table with us. In our tradition, the altar table is placed in the North, but being the practical people that we are, the huge tree stump served our needs perfectly, so we incorporated it into our witchy rituals.

The three of us enjoyed a couple of years trying different practices.

One night, during a ritual, we experimented with blood magic. Scarlet had just bought a new athame (black handled, double edged knife, which is worn sheathed on the cord tied around the waist in ritual), and wanted to cleanse and consecrate it for magical work.

Although our athames weren't to be used to cut anything tangible, she poo-pooed that idea, citing that was a modern-day ceremonial magician practice.

"Back in the olden days, witches would just use a sharp knife out of the drawer to cut herbs or whatever needed cutting," she declared. "There was none of this keeping a special knife that was never used to cut stuff."

During the full moon ritual, she washed her athame in water to cleanse it, sprinkled salt over for purification, wafted incense for protection, and then it was time to consecrate it with her own blood. Gritting her teeth, she slashed the blade across the palm of her hand.

Nothing happened. No blood.

She did it again, with no effect at all.

Scarlet, Meredith and I started to laugh. It looked so easy in the movies, but in real life, with a slightly blunt blade, Scarlet found it next to impossible to draw blood from her tough hand. Finally, we managed to slightly pierce her skin, and the blade was duly sprinkled with a small amount of her blood. Mission accomplished.

During other rituals we experimented by invoking unusual Goddesses and Gods, sometimes with eldritch effects.

One night, for example, we decided not to perform our usual circle set-up as we were feeling a bit lazy. We'd earlier agreed to invoke the blessings of Kwan Yin. She seemed like a lovely and protective Goddess, though we weren't too familiar with her history or cultural setting. Everything went well, until Meredith began suddenly screeching in a high-pitched voice, in what sounded like Mandarin.

Meredith only knows how to speak English.

Every hair raised on my body, and Scarlet and I looked at each other in shock. The two of us quickly stopped what we were doing, closed down the ritual and plied Meredith with food and water until she seemed normal again.

At other times, we performed one ritual in complete silence and a couple of rituals with no equipment at all, because after all the witch is the magic, not the tools that we use.

We celebrated Persephone's journey to and from the Underworld and opened magical doorways with Sheela na Gig.

On one memorable occasion, we did a ritual based around a labyrinth working. To create the labyrinth in an open field near to our circle space, I made the 'walls' out of toilet paper. It took three rolls to create the labyrinth, and it worked remarkably well as the papery boundaries shone bright white under the full moon. The design was based on the Labyrinth of Troy, and was 15 meters in diameter.

After we explored some mysteries associated with walking a labyrinth, we burnt the toilet paper 'walls' on a bonfire, and drank our mead while watching Troy burn. It was very satisfying indeed.

* * *

We decided to name our little group the Coven of SAW. The acronym SAW is one of our most closely guarded secrets. Yes, the name does have a specific meaning. As a joke, we would say it means Sexy Australian Witches, but it doesn't, really. Strangely, another Brisbane coven started up not long afterwards and called themselves The Coven of SOAR, which was kind-of annoying from a brand-identity perspective. We cheered ourselves up by declaring that we were the original and the best!

The Coven of SAW didn't take on any other members for nearly two years, so we had a delightful time. We experienced a huge surge of creativity and innovation, which included writing and performing experimental rituals together. We changed much of our standard ritual wording, simplifying the opening and closing of rituals down to the most fundamental basics, because we preferred to spend more time focusing on the magical working.

For example, we condensed the elemental quarter calls from seventy words down to nine words for each direction:

"Waters sweet, oceans deep. Powers Old. We call thee."
"Stone still, earthy hill. Powers Old. We call thee."
"Flame ablaze, sunny days. Powers Old. We call thee."
"Breeze light, airy flight. Powers Old. We call thee."
"Spirt bright, starry night. Powers Old. We call thee."

Eventually, despite the joys of belonging to a small coven, we experienced the practical challenges of needing to cancel scheduled get-togethers if one of us was sick or unable to attend. Also, after a couple of years of fun and experimentation it felt like it was time for another change. We decided to train some Novices, so that we could share our rituals with other interested people.

THE CIRCLE COVEN GENESIS

ONE BIG CHANGE for our small coven of three members was to change our name. This wasn't something we did lightly, as the name of a magical group is important. By naming something we are defining and shaping it to create an understanding of its nature.

One mundane impetus for the change was the release of the SAW horror movies, as we didn't want our coven to be associated with murder and torture. But the main reason was that we simply outgrew our name as it was no longer relevant to us.

After some meditation, we decided to rename The Coven of SAW anew to The Circle Coven. We chose this name as we felt that the shape of a circle was fundamental, as well as being the simplest and strongest shape able to be drawn continuously. A circle can be as large or as small as you like and, being the shape, it is, there are no rough corners to be rubbed off. We as witches do our spell-work in a circle. Seen from above, the top of a cauldron or a coffee cup are circles. Each is magical in its own way.

Although we were pleased with our new name, and despite having experience and a lot of enthusiasm, unfortunately the newly named Circle Coven wasn't too successful in retaining any new members for a long time. Over a few years, we had four different intakes of Novices, with a total of thirteen witches signing up. Not one of them is still a member of the coven.

On the plus side of things, we learnt a lot about people's personalities and how they interacted with other coven members. While some witches slipped away from coven membership quietly (for example the woman who attended two lessons then was never seen or heard from again), other coveners certainly left their mark on our memories.

For example, there was one man who was quiet and reserved, but suddenly, after a couple of months, decided that he should be the High Priest and run the coven. This was despite him only having theoretical knowledge gleaned from a variety of books with very little practical experience or ritual work at all.

Thanks, but no thanks.

Then there was a very flamboyant lad with highly developed psychic skills, who sadly couldn't take any directions from the three of us women. As mentioned previously, we are quite exacting in our ritual work and ask that all coveners comply with our practices. We know that there are many ways of performing a ritual, however when you work in a coven a shared understanding and methodology enables things to flow better.

I remember the night we requested that he cast a circle under our watchful teacher eyes.

We asked him to take the coven sword and perform the circle cast, which at its simplest requires walking around the boundaries of the ritual space, holding the point of the sword downwards to trace a certain shape.

A circular shape.

Sounds pretty simple, right?

To do this, the person starts in an East facing direction, walks around the edges of the defined circular space and finishes in the same location they started.

I'd never seen a circle cast like it!

He held the sword in his hand, and as he walked he drifted across the middle of the space, spun in wiggly spirals, moved back to the boundary, staggered outside of the boundary, and then finally concluded the so-called circle cast in the middle. He stood, head down, panting with the effort.

"Er, what was that?" I gently asked him.

His response was that he'd been buffeted by unseen forces. He tried to fight his way against them, but they were too strong, and he had to go with their demands. The energies were so powerful they threw him around the circle. He could hardly resist and could barely keep standing upright.

As the purpose of the circle cast is to define the different inner and outer worlds and keep away any malign forces, this was a complete fail…particularly as his efforts were critiqued by three experienced witches. None of us were aware of any evil influences or powerful spirits supposedly tossing him about.

We told him about our perspective, and after that night we never heard from him again.

To put a positive light on some of our previous male Novices, we had a calm and polite gentleman who joined us for a while. But a couple of months after joining, a new coven started up very close to his home, and his wife joined it. You could tell that this presented some difficulties for him, as although he was committed to us, the positive aspects of a local coven were very attractive to him. We talked with him, and all agreed that he should go with the other coven, although we were very sorry to see him leave.

Another lovely man simply had too many commitments when his garage band became famous.

Then there was the gorgeous young woman who diligently turned up for each meeting and ritual, listening with wide eyes to everything we said. Sadly, the first time we asked her to do some preparation work for a ritual, immediately her life got too busy and she quit the coven the very next day.

Speaking of lovely looking ladies, we sometimes have a giggle about a conversation that occurred during the early years of The Circle Coven. We'd just invited some new female Novices to join the coven, and two of them were sitting in the lounge room with one of our very attractive long-term members.

Wayne, Scarlet's husband, who was always quick with a jest, walked into the room and deadpanned, "So you've got to be good-looking to join the coven, right?"

At first, we didn't know what he was talking about, then burst into laughter when we realized that the two new women were also very attractive. It did seem (from a by-stander's perspective at least) that good looks were the main criteria for being accepted as a coven member!

After that, we like to joke about how you must be good looking to be a coven member, knowing full well that beauty comes in all shapes and sizes.

✳ ✳ ✳

To keep growing, a coven must take in new members to balance numbers when people leave. Funnily enough, over the years of training Novices with The Circle Coven, one thing we've consistently noticed is that the older group of Novices never seemed to particularly like the newest Novice group. Each preceding group seemed to think they were more hard-done-by than the newest arrivals, and that the newer members had to 'suffer less' and 'had it easier' during their training.

When you have three different intakes of coven members together, it sounded like a Monty Python sketch:

"What? You were allowed to walk in through the front door? We had to walk down the side of the house in darkness and try not to fall down the hidden steps!"

"Ha! You think that you had it tough? We had to wait six months to find out whether we were able to continue our training."

"We had to sit in the dark in the rain for five hours. You only had to be there for two hours."

In all fairness, I believe that we as coven leaders became a lot more relaxed over the years, so perhaps they were right. We were much tougher in the earlier days, and mellowed out with age, like a fine wine.

✱ ✱ ✱

After a few years of members coming and going, the status quo of The Circle Coven changed significantly when Jordan and Belladonna joined.

These two women were actively running open rituals and witchy events, but they were seeking formal training. Given their strong wills and determination, Scarlet and I were compelled to rise to their challenge, and thus the new Circle Coven was truly reborn.

Jordan and Belladonna took their coven training very seriously. They were completely committed and dedicated to learning what we had to teach. Because of this, they found it difficult occasionally to know when Scarlet and I were simply joking around and when we were imparting profound knowledge. And of course, some profound knowledge is seeded within what appears to be a joke, so it's understandable that occult wisdom can be difficult to differentiate from a simple bit of humor.

For example, we found out about a year after they'd joined that they'd been diligently washing their robes in freshly caught rain water and crystallized rock salt. Every time it rained, they would rush outside with a bucket, and save this water until it was needed after the next ritual, because that is what they thought they had to do. The rock salt also made their robes fade quite quickly to a pinkish color.

There was a moment of puzzled silence from Scarlet and myself. We then explained that no, we weren't being serious about that method of cleansing ritual robes. When our own robes required washing we popped them into the washing machine with some detergent. We couldn't abide people with stinky or stained robes, and liked ours washed properly.

I'm not sure if the two of them continued in their diligent robe-washing practices; but I know they were pleased to learn that there were other options available.

I believe that Jordan and Belladonna wanted us to appear as great and worthy Wise Ones on a pedestal, benignly dispensing occult wisdom. They wished for High Priestesses and Wise Teachers they could be proud of!

Contrary to this, at that time, we didn't even call ourselves High Priestess. We tried very hard not to be Wise Ones on a high pedestal, as falling off a pedestal can be quite painful, literally and metaphorically. It's far better to keep one's feet firmly on the ground and maintain a sense of humility and humor.

A WOMEN ONLY SPACE

THERE WERE MORE POSITIVE CHANGES to coven membership, which included Vivien joining the coven the Novice intake after Belladonna and Jordan started. Years later she was to become co-High Priestess of the coven.

In the mysterious way that the Universe balances things out, this marked the time that our dear Witchy-Sister Meredith decided she needed a break from the coven. Her passion for witchcraft had waned as she became more engrossed in creating a new handicrafts business. Scarlet and I were sad to see her leave, though our friendship continues to this day.

After Meredith resigned from the coven, Vivien, Belladonna, Jordan, Scarlet and myself made a momentous change. We decided that our membership would be restricted to women and we would no longer accept male Novices.

Becoming a women-only coven was one of the best decisions we ever made for The Circle Coven. We'd had a few issues with the two men who had most recently joined. They were tardy with completing the required Novice course tasks, and sometimes they didn't turn up for a meeting without letting us know beforehand. One of them – the non-attendee – simply drifted away and we never contacted him again. The other one had some relationship issues that were causing him some grief, and he tearfully took permanent leave from the coven.

So, there we were that fateful night, five slightly cranky women witches sitting around feeling annoyed about these latest experiences. That night, we collaboratively decided that although we had men in our lives (husbands, sons, partners, brothers, friends and fathers) whom we loved, we wanted to keep the coven as a space for women only.

We don't hate men. We like men. And we would not knowingly let any women join who felt strong anger towards males, as we do not wish to be a refuge for men-haters.

Bigotry and intolerance for others based on gender or sexual preference is not acceptable to us. In our rituals, we have a God candle and a Goddess candle on the altar, and give reverence to the masculine aspects as well as the feminine aspects of Deity. We recognize that there are many ways of understanding gender apart from polarity or a binary system, despite our usual coven traditions. But we agreed that our coven would only accept women members from now on.

Changing to a women-only coven certainly changed the dynamic of the group. Members feel freer and more open about sharing experiences. Some of our conversations are extremely ribald or include in-depth discussions about bodily functions or sexual experiences. We are able to explore and celebrate our feminine mysteries in a very safe environment, without the minefield of cross-gender sexual attraction. We also spend time working through the cultural issues that are peculiar to women.

For example, a common mentality we often come across is the practice of women, particularly older women, putting themselves down ("Oh I'm not very good at that!"), as if they are of low worth. We tell our new members that, in the company of coveners, belittling oneself is not necessary or required. You don't have to make yourself smaller, or less important, or appear less intelligent to 'fit in'.

As your sister-covener, I like you fine just as you really are, and we all appreciate your strength, power, and direct words and actions. There is no need to be girly or submissive to be part of the coven. We like your rawness.

Another coven culture we promote is encouraging our members to move towards a state of personal authenticity; whatever that means for the individual. What is authentic for one person can differ radically from what is genuine, or true, for another. The journey to being truly authentic can be a tough one, and we create 'space' in the form of acceptance and tolerance during that unfolding.

As part of that, the Circle Coven supports a culture where it is acceptable to express strong emotions – sorrow, pain, frustration, anger, delight - and to name and own these powerful feelings. This can, of course, be very confronting for those women with years of suppressed anger hidden behind a pleasant and amicable façade, but it is an important phase in the alchemical process of self-actualization.

After the coven adopted the decision to only include women, our bad luck with finding and retaining new Novices changed. Almost by magic, we were approached by large numbers of wonderful women who wished to join us. These women were bright, creative and committed, and many of them stayed for years and years with the coven. For about a decade, we had so many long-term members that we had to wait until they moved away from the city before we could take on new Novices.

On a seemingly mundane level, when we decided to become a woman-only coven, we also decided to change the color of the robes we wore in ritual. For years, we and many other Queensland Pagans wore robes of black, with ours having the addition of silver trim for females and gold trim for males.

"I'm sick of black," Scarlet bluntly put it.

Fair enough then, so what color robes shall we wear? The discussion went pretty much as follows:

Belladonna felt that navy blue reminded her too much of school uniforms and associated bad memories.

White would show the dirt, and be difficult to keep clean.

Another local coven wore green robes, so that was out.

Purple was over-used by New-age types.

Tartan would be too Scottish.

Orange did terrible things to my complexion.

So that left…um… red.

OK, so let's wear red robes!

Red represents the color of blood, of life, and of women's mysteries. In the archetypal triad of Maiden, Mother and Crone, red is the color of the generativity and creativity relating to the Mother, while white is assigned to the youthful Maiden and black to the wise and mature Crone.

Red is quite a confronting color; there is very little subtlety associated with bright red! Therefore, this color fit us perfectly.

We love our bold and courageous red robes. Our robes are made from a thick 100% cotton material, and are deliberately sewn to be loose and baggy.

Some women have a bit of difficulty with wearing a baggy robe, wishing their robes to appear flattering and conforming more to their shape. Soon they soon realize that it is a lot more practical to wear a robe with a generous amount of skirting to allow easy movement. A loose robe also allows one to sit down cross-legged with modesty and decorum.

Funnily enough, years ago in The Coven of the Enchanted Cauldron, Scarlet and another couple of coveners nearly sent our High Priest Connor into gibbering frustration by creating their robes from beautiful medieval gown patterns, adorned with ribbons, with low cut bodices and tight-fitting sleeves that flared out into extreme hanging lengths at the end. One witch even needed to tie knots in the end of her long sleeves to stop them dragging on the ground.

Poor Connor just couldn't comprehend their need to look 'pretty'. He soon set us all straight regarding the design of proper and practical robes.

According to Connor, robes need to be loose to allow for unrestricted movement, be high necked so your boobs don't fall out when you bend over, and long dragging sleeves are one of the most dangerous things you can wear in a witch's circle which includes naked candle flames.

Now Scarlet is one of the loudest advocates for: "This is how our robes should look, and this is what they will look like! And they will be shapeless and baggy. "

So shapeless and baggy – and red - our robes are.

INITIATION AND WOMEN'S MYSTERIES

AFTER MANY YEARS STUDYING the witch's arts, teaching other witches and learning as much as we could, Scarlet and I decided that it was time for us to undergo Third Degree Initiation. This wasn't a decision that we made lightly or frivolously. But it at last it seemed appropriate, and we finally felt ready to take this significant step along our spiritual path.

By then we could no longer call our group a Wiccan coven, particularly as we did not have any males in the coven. We were proudly eclectic, synthesizing pre-Christian pagan practices with ceremonial magic, intuition, modern culture and anything that worked! Therefore, we knew that our initiatory pathway needed to flow along these same lines.

We did a lot of consultation and questioning. Our ex-High Priest, Connor, provided us with advice, as did our ex-High Priestess Rhea. We talked to others running degree-based covens. But most importantly, we meditated and asked for guidance from the Universe, the Inner Worlds and the Gods.

Inspiration blossomed and the overarching theme for the Rites of Passage for The Circle Coven appeared. It was laughingly obvious, with the benefit of hindsight.

Being a women-only coven, we spend time exploring mythology and esoteric knowledge that linked with the feminine gender. Although we include masculine archetypes and deities in our shared coven rituals, it seemed quite natural to have a stronger emphasis on feminine archetypes and their application into spiritual life.

Many Western mystery traditions honor three aspects of feminine pre-Christian deity in the guise of Maiden, Mother and Crone. Historically, there is evidence of triple Goddess worship for over 2000 years in European and Aegean cultures. Robert Graves' book The White Goddess has also strongly influenced and inspired the neo-pagan understanding of a triple Goddess.

Slightly contrarily to this, our coven honors four, instead of three, different aspects of the Divine Feminine; Maiden, Mother, Crone and the Silent One. These aspects relate to phases of the moon as well as to internal and external life cycles.

The Maiden aspect relates to the archetype of the Goddess as a youthful girl, full of promise, laughter, optimism and innocence. We align the Maiden with the color white, flowers and the Spring ritual of Imbolc. She is associated with the waxing moon, when the moon is a crescent shape, slowly growing larger and fuller in her journey towards maturity.

The full moon is the representation of the Mother archetype. The Mother is associated with the ampleness of human experience, of maturity, fertility and creativity. The essence of Mother-hood doesn't require the actual birth of a physical child, as we can nurture, heal and fiercely protect without growing a baby within us.

Creating artwork, growing a garden, fostering animals or acting as a community volunteer are other aspects of the Mother archetype. The color of the Mother is red, being the color of life's blood and passion.

The waning moon, as it decreases in brightness and fullness, relates to the Crone. The Crone is the menopausal wise woman who holds the memory of the tribe. She is rich in experience although her body is no longer fertile. She can be irascible, and has few pretenses. She no longer needs please anyone else but she may choose to provide the love and continuity that the tribe needs to stay strong.

In the Circle Coven, we honor a fourth face of the Goddess, she of the dark moon. The dark moon phase is those nights when the moon is not illuminated by the sun; a time of pause between full moon cycles. We call her The Silent One. Within her, all possibilities and potentialities of the Maiden, Mother and Crone are cradled, yet she is not these. She is a Goddess of the secret ways, of whom little can be spoken.

There is no 'rule' that these aspects of the Goddess are specific to biological ages. There are young women who exemplify Cronehood despite their comparative youth, as well as mature women who enact a childlike wonder and delight in not acting their age. Some women, despite being in the middle of their fertile years and with multiple children can demonstrate the qualities more associated with the Maiden or the Crone.

Having said all of that, it is a useful paradigm to consider the aspects of the Goddess in relation to women's ages, particularly during transitions, such as from carefree youth into maturity, or from child-rearing days into cessation of menses.

Being a female-only coven, we often immerse ourselves in rituals and workings that link to the moon phases as well as to women-centric myths and archetypes to help us explore our social, magical, spiritual and embodied experience as women. Deeply exploring the divine feminine can be literally life changing.

It is into this system that we weaved into our Rites of Passage for the coven.

The Dedication Ritual links, of course, to the Maiden. This is the time of youth and new beginnings. Dedication welcomes the fledgling witch into her tribe.

First Degree Initiation is associated with the archetype of the Mother, and this is when the work really begins. This Degree is associated with teaching, and actively helping others.

The Crone oversees the Second Degree Initiation, and we ask her to bring us the wisdom and insight that we seek during this phase of our journey.

Therefore, Third Degree Initiation in our coven is guided by the deep-in-darkness Silent One, the fourth face of the Goddess. Third Degree Initiation marks completion of the cycle, and begins us again on the spiral of possibility.

The outward symbolism of the Third Degree saw Scarlet and I exchanging our well-worn blue cords for a new red cord. Perhaps of greater significance is that fifteen years after joining my first coven, I was finally endorsed as High Priestesses.

TEACHING NEW WITCHES

I AM PASSIONATE ABOUT training and education. During our transition into The Circle Coven as it is today, we re-crafted our old Novice curriculum to suit our new needs. As part of this process, I sat down with pages and pages of photocopied, handwritten and manually typed notes from the old Coven of the Enchanted Cauldron days, with towering stacks of books nearby for reference, and typed for hours and hours.

After days and days, taking breaks only for the mundane aspects of life such as work and sleep, my shoulders ached and my eyes blurred. But at last it was done.

Each document was lovingly formatted the same way, with an emblem of a Celtic knotwork circle in the top right corner and a light dotted border around the outside, because having thick heavy page borders chews through printer ink very quickly when you are printing out multiple pages. This is a lesson in Practical Witchcraft 101: how to cut down printing costs.

We also reworked the old year-long, weekly training course leading to First Degree Initiation into eight face-to-face, practical group lessons, supported by a theory-based workbook.

I admit that I cringe slightly when I look back over our documents from the early years. But at the time, each page was eagerly read and absorbed by our Novices, despite some dubious grammatical mistakes. And, of course, there was the infamous picture in our lesson pack of how to set up an altar, which had the candles located in the incorrect position. This confused Circle Coven Novices for many years!

As there is now so much information which is easily revealed by a Google search, we removed a lot of the generic content from the material, and refined it to reflect our coven practices in a more precise manner. We know that our coven practices are not the 'only' or the 'right' way of doing things. There are many different systems and traditions, with more re-discovered each year. But what we do as a coven is OUR way of doing things, refined through experimentation and what worked for us.

Sometimes we find a better way of doing things or learn new information, and we quickly include that into our practices. We try to balance discipline and structure with being dynamic and experimental. Of course, some new techniques don't work perfectly the first time – or at all – but trying new things is worth the risk of potential failure.

Our Novice training program includes a range of required activities that we half-jokingly call 'homework.' Watching how Novices challenge themselves to complete the homework is one of my favorite things about the training program. Our witchy homework isn't dry and boring theoretical stuff. We deliberately chose activities to enhance a creative and trans-rational style of learning.

As adults, it's really easy to neglect the creative arts in our everyday 'busy-ness' of life. Creating poetry or art, or crafting something made-by-hand brings so many non-tangible rewards. When we are fully engaged in the process of creating something, our hearts sing and we move into a different flow of time. Witchcraft is as much as about Science (rational thought and discrimination) as it is about Art (imagination, beauty, emotion). We need both.

This quote attributed to Pablo Picasso sums it up nicely: *"Art washes away from the soul the dust of everyday life."*

It's fascinating to watch how each successive group of The Circle Coven's Novices exceed the previous standards of homework. In the early days, a few pictures cut from a witchy magazine and stuck onto a piece of paper was the status quo. But as the years went by, the quality became higher and higher.

Some witches spent literally days and days preparing their homework, and the results are extraordinary. Some of the work created by Novices deserves to be published or on display in a gallery.

We don't judge homework based on how many hours were spent making it. The process that the witches experience in creating their homework projects is far more important than hours spent or artistic talents. For some Novices, the homework requirements caused a major breakthrough in their thinking as they initially doubted their artistic or creative abilities:

"Whatever I make will be terrible. I'm so bad at this."

"I can only draw stick figures. My hare looks like a donkey. Please don't laugh."

"I'm hopeless at writing poems."

But along the way, something amazing happens. The Novices start the tasks and usually find that they love the process of creation. Some go on to continue their creative endeavors, by making hand-crafted soap, or beading, or painting pictures for friends.

One of the first Novice homework tasks is writing a poem on the topic of 'what does it mean to be a witch'. But there is a twist in the tale. The poor Novices do not know that after they write their poem, they have to read it aloud to the other coveners at the next lesson!

For some people, this is very confronting, as it's one thing to craft a poem and a completely different matter to present it verbally to the world. However, reading one's poetry aloud is a powerful method to overcome feelings of self-consciousness. It's a cathartic experience, and we continue to build upon it as we learn to perform rituals together.

New and old members come together for the practical lessons during the Novice training. As well as sharing information, these lessons assist the Novices to learn about coven expectations and culture, or 'how we do things around here'. Not everything is written down in a rule book, and it's always enjoyable to learn from and with others.

The initial face-to-face lessons of the Novice course include exercises to sense and raise energy, hands-on chakra work, chanting activities, how to participate in a ritual, and of course spell-craft. For our coven, these are the essential 'must know' teachings that Novices need to learn before participating in a coven ritual.

Alongside all of that, we provide support for each other. Each meeting, we talk about what has been happening in our mundane as well as spiritual lives, because they are both connected. We celebrate birthdays, commiserate when spouses are trying our patience and provide problem solving advice when it's required. We also enjoy sharing jokes and laughing. Often the sound of our combined cackling can be heard wafting off into the night air during our get togethers.

AN ANNUS HORRIBILIS

EVER SINCE WE CREATED THE CIRCLE COVEN, I said that if Scarlet resigned from the coven, I would leave as well. We were a good team together, and relied heavily upon the support of each other. Our qualities were well balanced; while I tended to over-think things, she would leap in with intuitive decisiveness. Other times, I would curb some of her more extreme eccentricities. We trusted each other completely.

Then that fateful event finally happened.

After four years of University study, Scarlet started her mid-life career change to become a primary school teacher. She knew that the first year of teaching would require many additional hours of work at night and on the weekend. Her children were still young and her husband sometimes worked away during the week, so there were many compelling reasons why she made the call to leave the coven.

I cried for the whole day when she confirmed her decision. I felt overwhelming feelings of grief, and knew that the best thing for me to do was not to fight these feelings. That day, I did my housework with tears rolling down my face. Fortunately, my young children were too absorbed in playing with Lego bricks to notice my distress.

Synchronically, a fortnight previously I received a promotion at work which required me to work longer hours. I, too, was exhausted from balancing work, family and coven responsibilities. After easing through my tears and sorrow at Scarlet's decision, I also decided it was time for me to let go of running the coven.

Although Vivien had been heavily involved in leading the coven for the past year, she was growing her first baby, so she had no interest in taking on additional coven responsibilities at this time. The three of us met, and decided to offer the banner of High Priestess of The Circle Coven to Linda.

Linda was a well-liked coven member with a keen mind for administration. Although she was only thirty years old, her teenage daughter had started high school, and Linda was ready for some additional challenges. She was thrilled to be asked to take on the High Priestess mantle.

In keeping with our protocols, we quickly set a date for her Second Degree Initiation. We invited all coveners to attend a ritual immediately after Linda's Initiation, to witness the handover of leadership.

It was a poignant night, marking endings and new beginnings, joy and sorrow. Scarlet and I formally moved to the role of Coven Elders, where we would have minimal administration and leadership duties, but could attend whatever coven events we pleased, and provide advice when required. In other words, we had earned the right to participate in the fun stuff without the responsibilities.

To support Linda, Zuma moved into the Coven Maiden position, which she was very pleased about. One of the reasons that Zuma joined The Circle Coven was to create her own coven in the future. The Coven Maiden role would provide her with an opportunity to learn about the administration side of things. Although Zuma was twenty years older than Linda, she had been with the coven only a couple of years, which is another reason that we offered Linda the High Priestess role rather than the very enthusiastic Zuma.

The two women bonded closely in their new leadership positions, particularly as both were having relationship difficulties at the time. Each coped with their spousal issues in a different manner. Zuma worked through her relationship problems by having an affair as payback on her cheating husband, while Linda navigated legal disputes to try and claim share-custody of her daughter and the house. While the other coveners were slightly perplexed at the sudden change in leadership, they at first seemed quite accepting of it.

Sadly, what started off as a positive change became a terrible year for our tightly-knit coven, despite good intentions.

Linda went through hell that year, battling to leave her husband who was fighting back through his own lawyers. The stress that she was under in her personal life bled through into her leadership of the coven. She developed a sudden fiery temper, which was unleashed on the new Novices with very little warning. Her personality changed from being the gentle and patient woman we knew, into frustrated and impatient. Coveners were chastised like naughty children for any minor transgression, and reprimanded for seeking clarification regarding coven events.

I could see some of this happening from a distance, but I was too occupied with my new job in the meantime to spare the energy to provide much assistance. Linda and Zuma appeared to be competent women, and I was sure that things would work out all right; they just needed to settle into their new roles.

How wrong I was!

There was so much more going on behind the scenes that I wasn't aware of until months afterwards. Unbeknown to Linda, (or by Scarlet, Vivien or me), Zuma saw an opportunity for advancement, and secretly vied for leading the coven and the hearts of the new Novices. The mature Zuma played the role of "aren't I a nice-sweet-loving witch" against Linda's "meany-cranky-witch" persona.

Despite claiming Sisterhood to Linda, Zuma criticized Linda to the Novices and any other covener who spared the time to listen to her.

After nearly a year of watching coveners becoming unhappier, and Linda more dissatisfied, I finally got my act together and decided it was time for us all to talk through what was going on.

Linda, Vivien, Scarlet, Rhea and I met at our favorite pizza restaurant. After some social catching up, Linda began to talk about how difficult things were for her. Anxiously playing with her fork, Linda explained that she was experiencing financial difficulties due to the pending divorce, and that she needed to rent a cheaper house further away from the city.

She let us know that she didn't know how she would be able to continue to run the coven, as she would need to start working in the evenings to help bring in additional income.

After chatting for a while, I acknowledged it seemed time for me to return to the High Priestess role. That would allow Linda to step away from that role, move to a new house and potentially create a new coven which was local to her.

Linda seemed relieved by this decision, as well as delighted at the opportunity to create her own coven. In the meantime, she could attend whatever Circle Coven events she wanted to, so this all seemed like the perfect solution.

Scarlet was quite clear that she was happy with being involved with the coven as an Elder, and didn't want to step back into the hot seat of High Priestess. She was also still very busy learning her new role as teacher...and really enjoyed being an Elder, which was quite understandable. I too had enjoyed my time of freedom with minimal leadership responsibilities.

Fortunately, Vivien was willing to co-High Priestess with me, as her child was now toddling about. I was immensely relieved, as

Vivien was a very experienced and trustworthy witch. From practical experience, we found that doing the High Priestess role solo led to burnout, over time, and we weren't going to make that same mistake again.

We five women all walked away from that meeting feeling quite satisfied with the positive outcome for the continuity of the coven.

Unfortunately, Zuma wasn't satisfied. Linda let me know that Zuma was annoyed that she hadn't been invited to our meeting. As well, she felt put-out that she'd been downgraded from her Coven Maiden role because Vivien was returning into the co-High Priestess role, and we no longer needed a Coven Maiden.

It was then that we found that Zuma had been organizing activities with the Novices, without letting Linda know. Some of the Novices had been outspoken in telling Zuma how lovely and kind she was, particularly in comparison with the moody Linda. Zuma apparently saw herself as the protector of the new Novices, and perceived that Vivien and I were the interlopers to the current arrangements.

When I found what was happening, I asked to meet with Zuma, so we could chat, as things seemed to be getting out of hand. Zuma's behavior went against the ethos of our coven, and the situation could not continue as it was causing disharmony.

After talking things through, I let her know that she needed to take a break away from the coven, and let things settle down. During this time, I offered to support her with personalized training on a one-to-one basis, so that she could complete her Second Degree Initiation.

Within our coven structure, after Second Degree Initiation, Zuma would then be able to spread her wings and run her own hived-off coven. At the time, she seemed happy with that outcome, as forming her own coven was something she yearned for.

Once again, I thought that our coven was back on track, but once again I was completely wrong!

Unfortunately, Vivien, Scarlet and I had significantly underestimated how bad things had become. On my first meeting back as leader, I returned to a hot-pot of a dysfunctional coven on the verge of collapse. Instead of creating accord between members, Linda and Zuma had somehow played off covener against covener through a bizarre mishmash of misrepresentations and half-truths.

The newer members, as well as the longer term coveners, didn't know what to think, as Linda and Zuma had contacted each of them and complained that they had been unwillingly forced out of the coven. They also accused me of cursing them and sending them negative energy. Strange and accusatory emails and rambling text messages abounded.

It was kindergarten behavior at its worse, similar to what I'd seen years ago in the old Coven of the Enchanted Cauldron. This was another sad example of how bad group dynamics could become within a magical group.

Linda and Zuma's actions ruined relationships between most of the coveners, sowing seeds of distrust and fear. Added into this mix, a couple of the new Novices seemed to enjoy stirring up emotions and sharing falsehoods. A few of the coveners simply discounted the tales, but it caused a lot of heartache and confusion for others who were less sure about what was happening.

As co-High Priestesses, Vivien and I didn't want to share some of the uglier aspects of what was occurring, so we didn't say too much, which added to the confusion. Admittedly, sometimes we had no idea what was going on, which is kind-of embarrassing although accurate.

It was a terrible time. What was once a stable and supportive coven developed into a battle ground of cliques who distrusted each other.

Over the course of a year, more than half the coven members resigned. They couldn't recover from the stories that had been told, despite many being not true. It was very painful saying goodbye to some of my Sister Witches, but I admit I was glad to farewell a couple of the Novices who had enhanced the dramas.

Through all of this, Vivien, Scarlet and I decided that we would continue doing the Great Work of a magical group, and continue as the Gods wished us to do so, regardless of the adversarial actions of others. We did our best to ignore the unkind things said (and posted on social media) by witches who were once dear to us. We were determined to rebuild the coven anew.

It took over a year for the coven egregore (group soul) to recover.

But every cloud has a silver lining. The coven went from a large, impersonal group to a smaller one where everyone who remained was fond of each other and trusted their coven-sisters explicitly. At last, a lot wiser and fewer in number, we were ready for the next phase.

The year after the implosion of The Circle Coven, we held a re-Dedication ritual. During this ritual, attended by remaining members, renewed feelings of harmony and connection were expressed by everyone present. It was a special and magical night, filled with merriment and laughter.

As part of the re-Dedication ritual, Scarlet spoke aloud the names of the fifteen witches who were no longer members of the coven. At the calling of each name, she placed a pinch of frankincense incense onto the fire, and we watched the scented smoke waft away. Scarlet declared that each of these women were magically released from our coven, like smoke on the wind.

We all agreed: "So mote it be!"

I'm not a gardener, but I know that to grow a beautiful rose bush, it needs to be pruned and have piles of manure spread around the ground. To create new growth, dead leaves and branches must be removed. That necessary process happened within The Circle Coven, many years ago. And from those harsh experiences, we have again grown to be the dynamic, loving, vibrant community of witches that I feel privileged to belong to.

HIGHLIGHTS AND FUN TIMES

WHEN THE CIRCLE COVEN WAS at its largest in size, with ten to fourteen active members, we rocked along from meetings filled with laughter to ceremonies that touched the soul. There were many highlights which well and truly compensated for the rare times of difficulty.

Celebrating our rituals in a non-city setting is one highlight. Although most of our rituals occur in a suburban backyard, we deliberately celebrate a few times a year in wild bushland. On each occasion, there is something special about the night, partly due to the difference in venue, but more so because we felt invigorated by our uninhabited and natural forest surroundings.

All the rituals we perform at Slaughter Falls bushland are particularly special. Slaughter Falls, despite the uncanny sounding name, is a part of the 1500 hectares of natural parkland that makes up the Mount Coo-tha forestry reserve on the edge of Brisbane. Mount Coo-tha is the highest peak in Brisbane, and the name comes from the Indigenous Australian people's term for place of honey. There seems to be natural magic in that area which amplifies and enhances any spiritual ceremony.

We've enjoyed many Samhuin rituals around the base of the Mountain, sharing illuminating meditations and magical workings. Samhuin can be an unusual time of year, as it is a time when the veil between the worlds is thin. In keeping with these eldritch energies, we've done things such as invited random strangers to join in with our ritual, toasted each other with expensive champagne in alabaster goblets while sitting in mud, and positioned funky mini glow-in-the-dark-plastic pumpkin fairy lights as our circle boundary.

Occasionally a security guard would drive slowly past us as we gathered in the forest wearing our black cloaks, but they never stopped to question what we were doing.

Our rituals in the forest are a practical reminder that the grandest or most elaborate events don't always have the biggest impact. One summer, we'd planned an outdoors ritual at Mt Coo-tha, at our usual spot near Slaughter Falls. Although we had many active coven members at the time, for one reason or another, only four of us turned up on the night.

And what a night it was, as the water elementals won the fight for supremacy. But as it was only raining in light intermittent showers rather than a continual heavy downpour, we decided that the show must go on and we would proceed with our ritual regardless of the damp ground.

Over that waxing moon phase, we had been working with serpent energy. The very artistic Trinity had planned a ritual which focused on transformation, and in preparation she had modelled segments of a clay snake. Due to last-minute traffic delays, she was running late, so the other three of us walked the short distance along the track to our ritual site to set up candles and equipment while we waited for her.

Just as she arrived, scurrying along the path to us, the heavens opened, and it POURED with rain.

We got absolutely drenched!

Trinity's greeting words to us were an anguished cry of: "I've just had my hair done!"

For some reason that seemed to be hysterically funny, and we all burst into laughter as we stood there in the soaking rain. Then, as quickly as it started, the rain stopped. Suddenly the clouds parted and there in the night sky, in a tiny space between the dense clouds, the full moon was revealed. The moon literally beamed radiance down upon us. We stopped laughing and simply stood in awe, embracing an enhanced sense of the numinous.

✳ ✳ ✳

A couple of my favorite coven get-togethers included beads. Beading is great for those who love creating beautiful things or who like to learn by doing. It's a communal activity that can foster a sense of peace and contentment while making things together.

Crafting beaded creations is a rewarding witchy experience. Whether it's prayer beads, or a key chain or a necklace, the act of choosing and stringing the beads can either be reflective and meditative or social and relaxed.

In our first beading lesson, Ivy supplied wire, a carefully chosen supply of beautiful beads, wire snippers and all the accompaniments required for us to make our own 'pagan prayer beads'. The colors, shapes and patterns on the beads and associated hanging bits corresponded with the Celtic deities of Epona and Cernunnos.

Although I'm confident at drawing, sketching and creating artwork, I pretty much suck at physical crafts which require diligence and exactitude, so this beading session certainly pushed my comfort boundaries. But under Ivy's patient guidance we each created a lovely string of beads, which we were proud to hang from our cords in ritual.

Another beading session was a wonderful experience occurring during a coven weekend away facilitated by Ellen. She had been involved with beading for a while, and made her own beautiful glass blown beads. She bought along boxes and boxes of a huge range of beads crafted from natural crystal, glass, wood, plastic, coral and clay. It was like we'd been released into a wonderland of amazing tiny treasures!

Initially, the range was bewildering and overwhelming, and I will admit that some less-than-spiritual hoarding may have occurred by my sister witches. Fortunately, we had the gentle and persistent assistance of Ellen guiding us to make some simply stunning creations. She was very patient with us beginner beaders.

Her calm comment on being shown something in the process of being strung together incorrectly was a typical Ellen response: "That's just beautiful, but you are doing it all wrong."

✳ ✳ ✳

Social picnics are a rewarding way to spend time together. We like to invite close friends, children and family members, as a picnic can provide a relaxed opportunity for family to meet coven members. One of the most photogenic picnics was held at Beltane in a large, grassy public park.

A couple of our coveners were members of a local Morris dancing group that owned a very sizeable maypole. We raised the phallic pole the proper way and enjoyed dancing around and weaving the ribbons to tin whistle music courtesy of Jordan's partner. It was a very hot but pleasurable day and the children had a ball.

While the coven enjoyed the pagan aspects of the picnic, others simply enjoyed being out in the sun and laughing at being tangled up in the ribbons.

While we don't include a full-blown ritual during our picnics, we like to include a communal spiritual or magical aspect. For example, we create a mini altar on a central table, featuring a large silver goblet and flowers. Picnickers are encouraged to add gold coins or money to the goblet, and these funds are later donated to a worthy charity.

On another occasion, we've asked everyone to join together in a circle, and then step forward to give thanks for the previous year, and state what they would like to achieve in the next year. This is a lovely way to set intentions and express gratitude, with friends bearing witness. It's also a useful way of keeping track of goals and aims, if this activity is repeated at the same time each year.

✱ ✱ ✱

Examples of great Circle Coven experiences wouldn't be complete without mention of our 'famous' coven weekends away. We've had a few coven weekend adventures, either one or two nights, in various locations a few hours' drive away from our capital city. A weekend away is a magical opportunity to take a step back from the busy-ness of life and spend time with special people. With one notable exception, our coven weekends away have been collaborative, harmonious and nurturing experiences.

We usually include a ritual (though I do recall us deciding not to on a couple of occasions because we weren't in the mood for it at the time!), artwork, meditations, playing with tarot cards or other forms of divination, good food, lots of coffee, maybe an alcoholic drink or two and lots of conversations and laughter. It's a time to slow down and reconnect with people and the natural environment.

Occasionally we have incorporated a particular focus, such as the time we climbed a hill close to Gympie, which was believed to be a pyramid artefact created either by aliens or ancient Egyptians. During this escapade, we felt the strange energy fields of the place, then later celebrated with Absinthe while sitting under the stars.

Sometimes, strange and uncanny things have happened. Our first weekend away was progressing blissfully, featuring mountain air, shared activities, great food and companionship...until The Ghost appeared.

We'd had a few alcoholic drinks and were sitting on the rainforest-fringed veranda. One of the coveners was taking photographs, and talk turned to the appearance of orbs. Laughingly, we began calling loudly to the arcane orbs, inviting them to come and join us to be in our pictures.

Our photographer witch took another photo, then sat down suddenly with a look of shock on her face. Silently she showed us the digital image in her camera. In that photo was the eerie image of a gentleman wearing 18th century clothing and sporting long red sideburns on his face. His face floated in the glass doors between the veranda and the inside room. It certainly wasn't the reflection of any of the coveners.

The reactions to The Ghost were mixed. Some of the coveners just fell apart in hysterics, while others were fascinated.

"Let's take another photo and see if he's still there!" urged Jordan and me.

The more nervous among us felt that was a simply terrible idea and became quite upset at that suggestion. Among this mini chaos, one of the older witches calmly said: "Yeah, I saw him here earlier. We had a nice chat. He told me he was feeling a bit lonely."

※ ※ ※

Doing craft-work together is a fun coven activity, and the end results can later be used in shared rituals or private practice. On one memorable occasion, we created decorated rattles made from gourds.

Gourds are large, firm-shelled fruit that become semi-hollow as they dry. Beatrice chopped off the top of each gourd to scoop out the wet seeds inside, baked them to hardness in her oven, filled each gourd with rice (so that they made noise when shaken) and stuck the tops back on. When we arrived at her house, the gourds were waiting for us on a paper-covered table, with paints, paintbrushes, glitter and shiny items for us to play with.

We had a fabulous night decorating and painting the gourds according to our different levels of artistic ability. From certain angles, some gourds appear similar in shape to weirdly-shaped male genitalia, hence there was a lot of ribald comments which would be inappropriate in genteel company. The night inspired a lot of bad punning, along the lines of:

"Aren't our gourds gourdgeous?"

"Well that is gourd news."

"Oh, my Gourdess. And praise to the Gourd."

"We had a gourd time!"

We later used the gourds in rituals, including rain-summoning ceremonies, and they lasted for many years until we finally burnt them in a glorious bonfire one Samhuin night.

DIVINATION

FORTUNE-TELLLING, SOOTH-SAYING, tarot cards, runes and astrology. These words and deeds are intrinsic to the practice of modern witches. Many people love to know what lies beyond the thick shimmery curtain that screens us from glimpses of future life events. Witches dare to quickly tweak that veil aside, and share the information received to provide guidance or helpful advice.

After a bit of trial and error, most witches find there are certain divination tools they prefer using rather than others. For example, my first love was tarot cards and they are still my preferred 'go to' tool for divination. I've tried using the rune stones, but found them abrupt and too straightforward in comparison to the nuances of tarot cards. The throwing bones were fun but didn't really inspire me, and using a pendulum is very good for certain things, but limited when a complex divination reading is required.

There are seventy-eight cards in a standard deck of tarot cards. Each card contains a wealth of symbolism for the reader to interpret, including colors, numbers, mythology, astrology and alchemy. When laid out in a spread, the relationships between cards are interpreted to provide insights for the person involved. As well as a divination tool, the versatile tarot cards are invaluable as a tool for reflective meditation or personal insights, which is another reason that I love them.

As for the oft-repeated 'wisdom' that you must receive your first deck of tarot cards as a gift from someone else, well I think that's utter nonsense. If you want a deck of tarot cards, don't wait around to receive it, or blatantly hint to a loved one that you'd like a deck purchased on your behalf; simply buy them for yourself.

I purchased my first deck over thirty years ago, in Alice Springs. They have travelled round the world with me several times, and I still use them. I don't think self-purchasing the cards makes them any less effective or accurate!

We've had a few extremely talented astrologers in the coven, and I've experienced the surprisingly accurate horary application of astrology, but despite many attempts over the years I still find it difficult to remember the different houses and meanings. Usually when faced with an astrological chart I tend to go, "Oh look at all those crisscrossing lines," rather than receive any profound insights. Interpreting astrology is just not my thing. Fortunately, Vivien is always swift with her detailed astrological insights, which allows me to maintain my relative ignorance in this area. Thanks, Vivien!

On the other hand, I enjoy numerology. Numerology can be used as a quick divination technique. For example, adding up someone's day, month and year of birth to arrive at a single digit provides a snapshot of their personal characteristics.

But what sings to one person doesn't necessarily sound as sweet to another. While I really enjoy incorporating basic numerology into my divination practices, Scarlet is perturbed by numerology. Her eyes become blank and she tells me she wants to put her fingers in her ears and say, "la la la" whenever I give a lesson on numerology.

Sometimes the temptation is just too great, and she does put her fingers in her ears and sing, "La la la!"

Other systems I've used and like include the Druid Animal Oracle set by Philip & Stephanie Carr-Gomm, which are beautifully painted by Will Worthington, as well as the Celtic Tree Oracle by

Liz and Colin Murray. The Goddess Oracle by Lucy Cavendish is another favorite of mine for offering gentle insight into a situation. There is a plethora of decks and sets out there and sometimes it's difficult to stop at a single set. One covener was an avid collector of tarot decks, and had at least one hundred of them, stored lovingly in wooden boxes.

※ ※ ※

We frequently hold get-togethers for coveners and interested friends, focusing on divination practices. After walking up the steep, creaking and narrow stairs to the private room at a local pizza restaurant, we would order food then participate in an activity we half-jokingly call 'speed tarot.'

Speed tarot, like speed dating, involves giving or receiving a super-quick divination reading of only of a few minutes' duration. It's a valuable way to learn to do a reading in a noisy, congenial setting. It's also a lot of fun. Speed tarot helps to improve our reading skills, as the supplicant can provide the reader with immediate feedback on the divination, and there's less pressure on the reader as no money crosses hands.

Another enjoyable activity for a group is to practice locating objects using a pendulum. Some people like to buy a genuine crystal pendulum that has been sanctified and blessed by a spiritually-minded person, and these can indeed be beautiful creations.

We find using a pendant on a neck-chain works just as well as a store-bought pendulum. It's super practical, and you'll rarely be without this nifty tool. A piece of string tied through a ring is another cheap and easily transportable alternative.

Immediately before asking the questions you want answered with the guidance of your pendulum, spend a short amount of time calibrating or 'tuning into' your pendulum. Hold the string/chain between your thumb and forefinger and use the other hand to immobilize the bob end.

Say to your pendulum: "Please show me YES."

Release the bob end, and within a few moments you will notice the pendulum deliberately moves either in a circular or a back and forward motion. Once again, still the bob end before releasing it, this time saying: "Please show me NO."

What usually occurs then is that the pendulum moves in a different way to the previous swinging motion, giving you the metrics for a 'yes' or a 'no' response using your pendulum. If you don't succeed the first time, simply try again, or try a different type of pendulum.

Now comes the fun bit: experimenting with your pendulum to find items! The following activity requires a helper who isn't participating in the pendulum activity, and is willing to place an object in a secret location in the room of a house, or in a park.

Using a paper-based aerial map or plan, hold your pendulum above it, slowly moving your hand above and across the page. The user needs to watch the pendulum closely for a 'yes' signal, or unusual motion over a certain location on the map. After everybody has a turn, and marks the spot on the page where they believe the hidden item is located, the assistant reveals the true location of the object.

Psychometry is another divination skill that is enjoyable to practice with a group of people. There are a few ways to do psychometry, but the best 'blind' test is for each person to place a piece of jewelry – or perhaps a favorite item that they use every day – into an envelope. The strangest item I've seen included was a feather from a dearly loved pet bird!

Each envelope is then passed around from person to person, who holds the item through the envelope and tries to tune into images, sensations or messages that arise in relation to the item. Participants then write down their flashes of insight and inspiration on the outside of the envelope, before passing it onto the next person and receiving a new envelope in turn.

When the envelopes and items have been passed around to everyone, one by one the envelopes are opened to reveal the objects inside. This provides an opportunity for the owner of the jewelry or item to validate and give feedback to the group regarding what had been written on their envelope. Sometimes the answers are riotously funny, and sometimes uncannily accurate. But this activity provides a wonderful opportunity to practice your skills and check how accurate you are with the support of others.

MONEY MOJO BAG SPELL

WITCHCRAFT 'R' MAGIC AND SPELLS. Spell craft can be as simple as lighting a candle and speaking a few words of intention, or as complex as performing a group ritual using loads of equipment and detailed wording. Both ways are equally effective, but I personally enjoy joining with other people to craft a magical spell.

The Circle Coven has a favorite money spell, which we have performed a few times over the years. Some witches believe you shouldn't do magical workings for yourself, but we disagree. We have no issues or concerns about performing a money spell when finances are tight. On the other hand, we believe that when finances are hearty, it's equally as important to give back in some way to a cause, charity or person who needs some additional help.

We've had some tangible successes with this spell, as members have accomplished a range of great outcomes such as winning a $3000 media package, money mysteriously appearing in the bank account, a sudden job offer with increased remuneration or an unexpected refund on a bill.

The spell has quite a few components in it, so it nicely demonstrates the use of magical correspondences.

Prior to performing this ritual (or any ritual for that matter!), we put in a lot of groundwork pondering what we will do, how we will do it, and what resources we need. For this particular spell-working, we all agreed that we would create a mojo bag during the ritual.

Mojo bags, also known as spell bags, are great items to make as the culmination of a magical working. Essentially, a mojo bag is a small cloth bag, filled with specially chosen and energy-charged items, such as rock salt, herbs, crystals or coins. For this money spell, we chose green cloth for the bag and ribbon because of the association of the color green with abundance, fertility and finances.

Our Herbalist, Meredith, went to work and made an Attracting Wealth Oil, designed specifically for the ritual. She used grape oil as the base, and included essential oils of patchouli, cedar wood, vetiver and ginger. It smelt simply wonderful! The oil would be used to anoint our foreheads when we entered the circle, as well as to rub upon our mojo bags.

We deliberated about which Gods or Goddesses we would call upon to join us in our working. After flicking through a stack of mythology books, we decided to connect with the beneficial energy of the Goddess Mylitta. She is a Goddess of the moon and fertility worshipped in ancient Mesopotamia. Over the weeks prior to the ritual we learned of myth stories associated with her, and meditated to gain inspiration and connection with her archetypal aspects.

Finally, the night of the ritual arrived. We performed our usual ritual setup, and then sat on the ground in a circle, holding hands. In the middle of us a brazier smoldered, with a large silver (disguised as stainless steel) bowl nearby.

"Mylitta, I call to you to come and fill me with your power," we said in turn, and then began a simple chant using Her name repeated over and over again for a few minutes.

"Mylitta! Mylitta! Mylitta!"

Meredith had prepared bags of ground or dried herbs. As these were passed around the circle, she spoke aloud the magical properties of the organic substances; Ginger for love, money, success and power; Patchouli for money, fertility and lust; Vetiver for love, hex-breaking, money and anti-theft; Cedarwood for healing, money, purification and protection; Bergamot for money; and salt for protection, purification and grounding.

When we were handed a bag with one of the substances, we would smell the contents then take out a small amount to hold in our hands while we each declared aloud its purpose. This ingredient was then placed into the large silver bowl.

Silently, we shared around a small bag of silver coins and green crystals that we had previously collected and placed these one by one into the bowl.

Pre-cut green ribbons about 50cm long, and circles of green cloth about 15cm in diameter were then laid out around the silver bowl. Before the ritual these had been painted with the symbol of Jupiter, the pagan Roman god who governed commerce and finances.

Participants spent a short while to silently meditate on the wealth and riches this spell would bring them, and then it was time for energy raising.

We'd brought along a range of simple musical instruments and noise-makers, including drums, tambourines, gourds, clapping sticks and shakers, so picking up our instrument of choice we launched into our money-making chant.

Our chant was very simple:
"*Money, money come to me,*
As I do will, so mote it be!"

The simplest chants are often the best, because it's easy to get complex lines and words mixed up while dancing around the circle beating a drum. Our money-making chant is very catchy and never forgotten.

As the beating of the drum became more frenetic and our dancing became faster, we just cried out "Money! Money! Money!" continuously until the energy-charge peaked and "DOWN" was called. This was the signal for us to drop to the ground and focus our intentions and energy into the prepared items.

The spell was done.

After that sense of release, we quietly scooped up the contents of the silver bowl into the centers of the pre-cut cloth, drew up the edges to make a pouch, and tightly tied and secured the contents inside with a ribbon. Experience has taught us to tie our ribbons tightly and securely, as you don't want your mojo bag contents to trickle out unexpectedly. Another trick is to use a tightly woven cloth for the bag, for the same reason.

The symbols of Jupiter were traced onto the bags with one finger which had been dipped into the Abundance Oil, and the edges of the mojo bags were anointed to 'seal' the bags.

After creating a mojo bag, our practice is to wear it for the next seven days. Some witches like to use the ribbon ends to create a necklace, but simply popping the mojo bag inside your brassiere is a very convenient way of keeping it close to you. That way the smell of the scented oil gently wafts out, as a reminder of the spell. At night, I keep my new mojo bags under my pillow.

Usually after the initial phase of wearing and keeping magically charged spell-bags close, I tie the mojo bag under my bed frame for safekeeping. At one stage I had quite a few of these small bags tied down under my mattress, as I like to store them for a few years. Maybe the efficacy of the spell-work has passed, but I keep them as memento until I feel completely ready to disperse the little bags.

When I'm ready, I will either untie or cut the bag, and let the contents spill out. I return the herbal and natural substances to the earth, thanking the local devii (nature spirits). Any coins or physical objects are placed back into circulation. I will either burn or bury the bag itself, according to my whim at the time.

There are quite a few cotton bags slowly decomposing in our back yard, hidden in strategic positions so my husband doesn't accidentally dig them up while he is gardening. He's now used to leaving shiny stones and crystals where they lie among the plants, knowing that these are often the end-products of magical spells.

# LIVING WITCHERY

EPILOGUE: THE CIRCLE

THE NATURE OF A CIRCLE is to be continuous. A year after starting to write this book, I left my warm home to celebrate in ritual with my coven sisters. Despite the chilly weather, we met outdoors clothed in our robes of red, covered in thick cloaks.

We chanted under the night sky and experienced the sense of the numinous before starting our magical working.

Our spell-work focused on the Cosmic Egg. Vivien drummed slowly as she led us on a guided meditation. She spoke the following words, based on a passage by Victor Hugo in Les Misérables:

> *You sit alone with yourself.*
> *Collected, tranquil, adoring.*
> *Compare the serenity of your heart with the serenity of the skies.*
> *Move towards the darkness.*
> *See the visible splendor of the constellations.*
> *Sense the invisible splendor of the Gods.*
> *Open your soul to the thoughts which fall from the unknown.*
> *Offer up your heart to the flowers of the night.*
> *Inhale their perfume.*
> *Be alight like a lamp in the center of the starry night.*
> *Expand your soul with ecstasy.*
> *in the midst of the universal radiance of creation.*
> *What is passing in your own mind?*
> *Something departs from you.*
> *Something descends upon you.*

All the mysterious interchanges of the depths of your soul with the depths of the universe.

Into our cupped hands Vivien carefully placed an ovoid object.

"In your hands you hold the power of the Cosmic Egg. All things that exist are within. Will you unleash inspiration? Gain perspective on your life? Connect with the Goddess? Or clear away obstacles? Pay close attention to whatever arises for you in this moment," she whispered to each of us.

Vivien instructed us to walk to each of the directional quarter points of the circle with our egg, and do the following:

In the East, state your intent;
In the South, channel energy to the egg;
In the West, connect or release your emotions as needed;
In the North, help your egg hatch;
Then, return to the center of our Circle in silence.

Each of us holds the power of our potential within us, like a personal Cosmic Egg. It's our choice how we nurture this, according to life's circumstances and our own Will.

Over the years, belonging to a witch coven has helped me realize my personal potential. From anxious Novice to confident High Priestess, it's been a remarkable journey. I've loved sharing it with every covener, regardless of whether we travelled together for a month or a life-time.

I send you blessings for your own journey, whatever form it takes, and wherever your path leads you

RECOMMENDED READING & BIBLIOGRAPHY

Budapest, Z. *The Holy Book of Women's Mysteries*. Wingbow Press, 1980.

Demarco, S. *There's a Witch in the Boardroom. Proven Business Magic*. The Modern Witch, 2003.

Carr-Gomm, P. & R. Heygate. *The Book of English Magic*. John Murray, 2010.

Farrar, J. and G. Bone. *Progressive Witchcraft*. New Page Books, 2004.

Farrar, S & Farrar, J. *A Witches' Bible: The Complete Witches Handbook. Phoenix Publishing*, 1996 (new edition)

Gardner, G. *Witchcraft Today*. Citadel Press, 2004.

Graves, R. *The White Goddess*. Farrar, Straus and Giroux, 1966.

Hall, N. *The Moon and the Virgin: Reflections on the Archetypal Feminine*. Harper and Row, 1976.

Hugo, V. *Les Misérables*, 1862.

Hutton, R. *Triumph of the Moon: A History of Modern Pagan Witchcraft*. Oxford University Press, 1999.

Jung, C.G. *Psychology and Religion: West and East*. Princeton University Press; 2nd edition. 1975. (P.131)

Leland, C. *Aradia or The Gospel of the Witches*. David Nutt, 1899.

Morgan. L. *A Deed Without a Name: Unearthing the Legacy of Traditional Witchcraft*. Moon Books, 2013.

Parma, G. (editor) *Crafting the Community*. Conjunction Press, 2009.

Parma, G. *Ecstatic Witchcraft*. Llewellyn Publications, 2012.

Starhawk. *The Spiral Dance*. Harper & Row, 1989.

Walker, B. *The Woman's Encyclopedia of Myths and Secrets*. Harper & Row,

www.ingramcontent.com/pod-product-compliance
Lightning Source LLC
Chambersburg PA
CBHW030259010526
44107CB00053B/1763